はしがき

　本書は第一学習社発行の英語教科書「CREATIVE English Communication I」に完全準拠したワークブックです。各パート1ページで，授業傍用と授業後の復習として役立つ練習問題のみならず，各レッスンの最後には総合問題も用意しました。また教科書本文のディクテーションも設けました。

CONTENTS

Part 1 教科書 p.10〜p.11 　　/54

A Write the English words to match the Japanese. 【知識・技能（語彙）】（各 2 点）

1. .... 图 身長 B1　　2. .... 图 体重 B1

3. .... 图 主義，モットー B1　　4. .... 图 失敗 B1

5. .... 图 競技連盟，リーグ B1　　6. .... 图 ピッチング，投球

B Choose the word whose underlined part's sound is different from the other three.

【知識・技能（発音）】（各 2 点）

1. ア．gr<u>ea</u>t 　　イ．k<u>ee</u>p 　　ウ．l<u>ea</u>gue 　　エ．t<u>ea</u>m

2. ア．<u>ch</u>ampionship 　　イ．<u>ch</u>ild 　　ウ．pit<u>ch</u>ing 　　エ．s<u>ch</u>ool

3. ア．br<u>ea</u>k 　　イ．g<u>a</u>me 　　ウ．h<u>ei</u>ght 　　エ．w<u>ei</u>ght

C Complete the following English sentences to match the Japanese.

【知識・技能（表現・文法）】（完答・各 3 点）

1. その赤ちゃんは約 1 時間泣き続けた。

The baby (　　　　) (　　　　) for about an hour.

2. 私の兄は昨年にアメリカの大学を卒業した。

My brother (　　　　) (　　　　) university in the U.S. last year.

3. あのレストランはおいしいスープを提供することで有名だ。

That restaurant (　　　　) (　　　　) (　　　　) serving delicious soup.

D Arrange the words in the proper order to match the Japanese.

【知識・技能（表現・文法）】（各 4 点）

1. 私の妹は海で泳ぐのを怖がる。

My little sister (afraid / in / is / of / swimming) the sea.

----

2. 彼女はプロのピアニストとしてデビューしたいと思っている。

She wants (as / debut / her / make / to) a professional pianist.

----

3. 彼の名前はレイモンドだが，友達は彼をレイと呼んでいる。

His name is Raymond, but (call / friends / him / his / Ray).

E Fill in each blank with a suitable word from the passage.

【思考力・判断力・表現力（内容）】（各 5 点）

1. Shohei's motto is "Keep trying harder. Don't be afraid of (　　　　)."

2. His team (　　　　) in the first game at Koshien.

3. He is very famous for being (　　　　) at both pitching and batting.

2

Part 2 教科書 p.12

/50

A Write the English words to match the Japanese. 【知識・技能（語彙）】（各2点）

1. .... 動 …を達成する A2   2. .... 名 子供時代 A2
3. .... 形 プロでない B2   4. .... 名 基礎 A2

B Choose the word whose underlined part's sound is different from the other three.
【知識・技能（発音）】（各2点）

1. ア. achieve   イ. childhood   ウ. coach   エ. machine
2. ア. able   イ. active   ウ. baseball   エ. basic
3. ア. enjoyed   イ. joined   ウ. played   エ. started

C Complete the following English sentences to match the Japanese.
【知識・技能（表現・文法）】（完答・各3点）

1. 私は英語のリスニングを向上させる努力をしなければならない。
   I have to (　　　) (　　　) (　　　) to improve my English listening.
2. ジョージは全員の中で最も速い走者だった。
   George was (　　　) (　　　) runner (　　　) all the members.
3. この地図のおかげでそこにたどり着くことができた。
   (　　　) (　　　) this map, I was able to get there.

D Arrange the words in the proper order to match the Japanese.
【知識・技能（表現・文法）】（各4点）

1. あなたが家を出るときまでには戻ってきます。
   I'll (back / be / before / leave / you) home.

2. その日が私たちの長い友情の始まりだった。
   The day was (friendship / long / of / our / the beginning).

3. 母はいつも私に自分の部屋をきれいにしておくように言う。
   My mother always (keep / me / my room / tells / to) clean.

E Fill in each blank with a suitable word from the passage.
【思考力・判断力・表現力（内容）】（各5点）

1. Shohei is the (　　　) of three children in his family.
2. He joined a local baseball team when he was (　　　) years old.
3. Shohei's father was a (　　　) of his team, so he taught him how to practice.

3

Part 3 教科書 p.14

/54

A Write the English words to match the Japanese. 【知識・技能（語彙）】（各2点）

1. .... 图 方法 A2
2. .... 图 目的, 目標 A2
3. .... 图 達成 B1
4. .... 图 シート, 一枚の紙 B1
5. .... 動 …を分ける A2
6. .... 形 中央の B1

B Choose the word whose underlined part's sound is different from the other three.

【知識・技能（発音）】（各2点）

1. ア. bro<u>th</u>er　　イ. me<u>th</u>od　　ウ. <u>th</u>at　　エ. <u>th</u>en
2. ア. de<u>ci</u>de　　イ. di<u>vi</u>de　　ウ. h<u>i</u>gh　　エ. <u>i</u>mportance
3. ア. c<u>oa</u>ch　　イ. g<u>oa</u>l　　ウ. l<u>o</u>cal　　エ. t<u>au</u>ght

C Complete the following English sentences to match the Japanese.

【知識・技能（表現・文法）】（完答・各3点）

1. 沖縄旅行の日を決めましたか。

   Did you (　　　　) (　　　　) a date for your travel to Okinawa?
2. それでは, クラスを6つのグループに分けます。

   Then, I'll (　　　　) the class (　　　　) six groups.
3. 彼の将来の目標は子供たちに水泳を教えることだ。

   His future goal is (　　　　) (　　　　) children swimming.

D Arrange the words in the proper order to match the Japanese.

【知識・技能（表現・文法）】（各4点）

1. 自分の考えをはっきりさせるのは難しいと思った。

   I thought that (difficult / it / make / my idea / to / was) clear.

   ----
2. 両親は一人暮らしをするという私の計画をよく思っていない。

   My parents don't like (by / live / my plan / myself / to).

   ----
3. 健康を保とうとするとき, 毎朝のジョギングが役立ちますよ。

   (can / every morning / help / jogging / you) as you try to stay healthy.

E Fill in each blank with a suitable word from the passage.

【思考力・判断力・表現力（内容）】（各5点）

1. Shohei's coach taught him a (　　　　) for achieving his goals and dreams.
2. You should write your final goal in the (　　　　) square of your Target Achievement Sheet.
3. Shohei (　　　　) the importance of writing down goals on paper.

4

Part 4 　教科書 p.16

A　Write the English words to match the Japanese.　【知識・技能（語彙）】（各2点）

1. ....　形 著しい B1
2. ....　图 進歩，進化 B1
3. ....　图 失望, フラストレーション B1
4. ....　图 やる気, モチベーション B1
5. ....　图 もと B1

B　Choose the word whose stressed syllable is different from the other three.

【知識・技能（発音）】（各2点）

1. ア．fail-ure　　　イ．fo-cus　　　　ウ．prog-ress（名詞）　エ．your-self
2. ア．frus-tra-tion　イ．im-por-tant　ウ．re-mem-ber　　エ．un-der-stand
3. ア．en-vi-ron-ment　イ．mo-ti-va-tion　ウ．pro-fes-sion-al　エ．re-mark-a-ble

C　Complete the following English sentences to match the Japanese.

【知識・技能（表現・文法）】（完答・各3点）

1. 先生は私たちに，スポーツの歴史を集中して学ぶように言った。

   Our teacher told us to (　　　　) (　　　　) studying the history of sports.
2. 夜中じゅう雨が降り続いた。その結果，川が濁った。

   It kept raining during the night. (　　　　) (　　　　) (　　　　), the river became dirty.
3. 夜更かしは病気につながることがある。

   Staying up late can (　　　　) (　　　　) sickness.

D　Arrange the words in the proper order to match the Japanese.

【知識・技能（表現・文法）】（各4点）

1. 私は誕生日にいとこにあげるプレゼントを探していた。

   I was looking for (a present / give / my cousin / to) for his birthday.

   ----
2. 私たちの仕事でよい進展が見られてうれしく思います。

   I'm glad that we (good / made / our work / progress / with).

   ----
3. 熱は氷を水に変える。

   (changes / heat / ice / into / water).

E　Fill in each blank with a suitable word from the passage.

【思考力・判断力・表現力（内容）】（各5点）

1. When he hurt his leg and couldn't pitch, Shohei focused on (　　　　).
2. He believes that failure can become the basis for (　　　　).
3. He thinks that it is (　　　　) to achieve big dreams.

5

Activity Plus 教科書 p.20〜p.21 　/54

A Write the English words to match the Japanese. 【知識・技能（語彙）】（各2点）

1. .... 動 …を選ぶ B2
2. .... 形 不可欠な B1
3. .... 名 メダル A2
4. .... 名 競争 A2
5. .... 形 前の B1
6. .... 名 困難 B1

B Choose the word whose stressed syllable is different from the other three.

【知識・技能（発音）】（各2点）

1. ア．jun-ior 　　イ．meth-od 　　ウ．ri-val 　　エ．se-lect
2. ア．ath-lete 　　イ．di-vide 　　ウ．hard-ship 　　エ．med-al
3. ア．bad-min-ton 　　イ．es-sen-tial 　　ウ．na-tion-al 　　エ．pre-fec-ture

C Complete the following English sentences to match the Japanese.

【知識・技能（表現・文法）】（完答・各3点）

1. 長い討議の後，タカシが学級委員長に選出された。

    After a long discussion Takashi (　　　) (　　　) (　　　) class president.

2. このホテルは，「トップホテルアワード2020」で3位になった。

    This hotel (　　　) (　　　) third in the "Top Hotel Awards 2020."

3. 高橋尚子選手は2000年のオリンピックで金メダルを獲得した。

    Naoko Takahashi (　　　) a gold medal in the Olympics in 2000.

D Arrange the words in the proper order to match the Japanese.

【知識・技能（表現・文法）】（各4点）

1. 子供がこの川で泳ぐのは危険だ。

    (children / dangerous / for / is / it / swim / to) in this river.

    ----

2. 滞在中に私を支えてくれたことに対して，私はホストファミリーに感謝したい。

    I'd like to (for / host family / my / supporting / thank) me during my stay.

    ----

3. 友人を得る唯一の方法は，自分が友人となることである。

    The (a friend / have / only / to / way) is to become one.

E Fill in each blank with a suitable word from the passage.

【思考力・判断力・表現力（内容）】（各5点）

1. Akane Yamaguchi was ranked (　　　) in the world in 2018.
2. Mima Ito's former partner for doubles is both her good friend and good (　　　).
3. Sota Fujii became a (　　　) when he was only 14 years old.

総合問題

Read the following passage and answer the questions below.

　　In my high school days, my coach, Hiroshi Sasaki, taught me a method for achieving my goals and dreams.　The method was the use of a "Target Achievement Sheet."　I believe that it is very important to decide (　1　) a goal and make it clear.

　　I (A)(how / make / teach / to / will / you) a Target Achievement Sheet.　First, divide a square (　2　) nine equal parts.　Then, write your final goal in the central square.　In (　3　) square around the central square, set small targets to achieve your final goal. My final goal was to become a professional baseball player after high school.

　　I (B)(down / learned / of / the importance / writing) goals on paper.　Writing down your goals can help you as you try to achieve (C)them.

1. 空所(1), (2), (3)に入る適切な語を選びなさい。　　　　　【知識・技能（語彙・表現）】（各4点）
   (1)　ア．in　　　　　イ．into　　　　　ウ．on　　　　　エ．to
   (2)　ア．by　　　　　イ．into　　　　　ウ．off　　　　　エ．out
   (3)　ア．all　　　　　イ．both　　　　　ウ．each　　　　　エ．some

2. 下線部(A), (B)の（　　）内の語句を適切に並べかえなさい。　　　　【知識・技能（文法）】（各4点）
   (A)　--
   (B)　--

3. 下線部(C)が指す具体的な内容を本文中から2語で抜き出しなさい。

   【思考力・判断力・表現力（内容）】（8点）

   (　　　　　) (　　　　　)

4. 本文の内容に合っているものをすべて選びなさい。　　【思考力・判断力・表現力（内容）】（完答・10点）
   ア．Hiroshi Sasaki was Shohei's coach in Major League.
   イ．Shohei's coach taught him the use of a Target Achievement Sheet.
   ウ．In a Target Achievement Sheet, you should set small targets in the central square.
   エ．Shohei gave up his final goal to become a professional baseball player.
   オ．It is helpful for you to write down your goals.

5. 次の問いの答えになるよう，空所に適切な語を補いなさい。

   【思考力・判断力・表現力（内容）】（完答・各6点）

   (1)　What method did Hiroshi Sasaki teach Shohei?
   　　── He taught him the use of a (　　　　) (　　　　) (　　　　).
   (2)　How many squares can you get for setting small targets to achieve your final goal?
   　　── I can get (　　　　) squares.

7

ディクテーション

Listen to the English and write down what you hear.

Part 1

You found some information about Shohei Otani on the Internet. You are learning about him.

Shohei Otani   Throws Right   Bats Left

Height 193 centimeters   Weight 95 kilograms

Date of Birth July 5, 1994   Hometown Oshu, Iwate Prefecture

Motto "Keep trying harder. Don't be afraid of (1.   )."

Personal History

    Shohei Otani began playing baseball when he was an (2.   ) school student. In his high school days, he played in the high school baseball (3.   ) at Koshien twice. In both tournaments, his team lost in the first game. After he graduated from high school, he joined the Hokkaido Nippon-Ham Fighters. In 2018, he made his Major League (4.   ). He is very famous for being good at both pitching and batting. People in Japan and the U.S. call him a "(5.   ) player."

Part 2

Shohei Otani always makes every effort to achieve his dreams. He gives us some useful hints for achieving our own dreams.

①   I am the youngest of three children in my family. I was active in my (1.   ), and I liked sports very much. I enjoyed badminton and swimming before I started to play baseball.

②   My father was a member of a (2.   ) baseball team, and my older brother also played baseball. I joined a local baseball team when I was (3.   ) years old. This was the beginning of my love for baseball.

③   My father was a (4.   ) of my team, so he taught me how to practice. He always told me to learn the (5.   ) of playing baseball. Thanks to his advice, I was able to become a better player.

Part 3

④   In my high school days, my coach, Hiroshi Sasaki, taught me a (1.   ) for achieving my goals and dreams. The method was the use of a "(2.   ) Achievement Sheet." I believe that it is very important to decide on a goal and make it clear.

⑤   I will teach you how to make a Target Achievement Sheet. First, (3.   ) a square into nine equal parts. Then, write your (4.   ) goal in the central square. In each square around the central square, set small targets to achieve your final goal. My final goal was to become a (5.   ) baseball player after high school.

6   I learned the importance of (6.   ) down goals on paper. Writing down your goals can (7.   ) you as you try to achieve them.

Part 4

7   What can you do to achieve your dreams? I have (1.   ) important things to tell you.

8   First, you should ask yourself, "What can I (2.   ) on now?" When I hurt my leg and couldn't pitch, I focused on batting. As a result, I made remarkable (3.   ) with my batting skills during that period.

9   Second, you should understand that failure can lead to (4.   ). Losing isn't the end. You should change your frustration into (5.   ). I believe that failure can become the basis for success.

10   Finally, you should remember that it is (6.   ) to achieve big dreams. You will need to make every (7.   ) and try hard to achieve them. Good luck!

Activity Plus

You found some information about young Japanese athletes and a professional on the Internet. You are reading about them and listening to them.
Young Japanese Athletes and a Professional

Akane Yamaguchi is a (1.   ) player. She was born on June 6, 1997. When she was in her third year of junior high school, she was (2.   ) as the youngest member of Japan's national badminton team. In 2018, she was (3.   ) first in the world. Her motto is "Enjoy playing every game."

It is important for you to do better than last year. Great efforts are essential.

Mima Ito is a (4.   ) tennis player. She was born on October 21, 2000. In 2018, she won three gold medals in Japan's national competition. Her former partner for doubles, Miu Hirano, is both her good friend and good (5.   ).

Thanks to my rivals, I'm able to focus on playing now. I want to thank my coaches, rivals, friends and family for supporting me during my hardships.

Sota Fujii is a (6.   ) *shogi* player. He was born on July 19, 2002. On October 1, 2016, he became a professional when he was only 14 years old. In 2018, he got the (7.   )-dan in *shogi*.

It is very important for me to keep finding the best way to win. The only way to experience being a champion is to become one, so I always make every effort to reach the top.

Part 1 教科書 p.26〜p.27 ／48

A Write the English words to match the Japanese. 【知識・技能（語彙）】（各2点）

1. .... 図 多様性，種類 B1　　2. .... 形 典型的な B1

3. .... 形 長距離の B2

B Choose the word whose underlined part's sound is different from the other three.

【知識・技能（発音）】（各2点）

1. ア．b<u>u</u>siness　　イ．d<u>i</u>sh　　ウ．t<u>y</u>pical　　エ．var<u>ie</u>ty

2. ア．conv<u>e</u>nience　　イ．exp<u>e</u>nsive　　ウ．r<u>e</u>staurant　　エ．sugg<u>e</u>stion

3. ア．cont<u>ai</u>n　　イ．st<u>a</u>tion　　ウ．tr<u>ai</u>n　　エ．tr<u>a</u>vel

C Complete the following English sentences to match the Japanese.

【知識・技能（表現・文法）】（完答・各3点）

1. 私の父は野球やサッカーなどのスポーツ観戦をするのが好きだ。

My father likes to watch sports (　　　　) (　　　　) baseball and soccer.

2. 私は来年の夏にカナダに行く計画をしています。

I am (　　　　) (　　　　) go to Canada next summer.

3. 学校へ行く前にマスクを付けなさい。

Put on your mask (　　　　) (　　　　) to school.

D Arrange the words in the proper order to match the Japanese.

【知識・技能（表現・文法）】（各4点）

1. 私はエスカルゴを食べてみたい。

(I / some / to / try / want) escargots.

----

2. もしイタリアに行ったら，ローマでピザを食べるといいよ。

If you visit Italy, (eat / in / pizza / should / you) Rome.

----

3. これらの料理は高校生によって作られました。

(by / made / these dishes / were) high school students.

E Fill in each blank with a suitable word from the passage.

【思考力・判断力・表現力（内容）】（各5点）

1. Lilly wants to try some bentos and asks for some (　　　　).

2. Each convenience store in Japan has a large section for bentos and you can choose one from a wide (　　　　).

3. Emily writes that we can buy our bento before (　　　　) and enjoy it on the train.

Part 2 　教科書 p.28 　/54

A　Write the English words to match the Japanese.　【知識・技能（語彙）】（各2点）

1. .... 图 電子レンジ B2
2. .... 图 弁当箱
3. .... 動 …を魅了する B1
4. .... 副 きちんと
5. .... 動 …を並べる B1
6. .... 動 …を含む B1

B　Choose the word whose underlined part's sound is different from the other three.

【知識・技能（発音）】（各2点）

1. ア．arr<u>a</u>nge 　イ．attr<u>a</u>ctive 　ウ．f<u>a</u>scinate 　エ．s<u>a</u>ndwich
2. ア．c<u>ou</u>ple 　イ．c<u>ou</u>sin 　ウ．enc<u>ou</u>rage 　エ．th<u>ou</u>ght
3. ア．br<u>ea</u>k 　イ．dr<u>ea</u>m 　ウ．m<u>ea</u>l 　エ．n<u>ea</u>tly

C　Complete the following English sentences to match the Japanese.

【知識・技能（表現・文法）】（完答・各3点）

1. ますます多くの人々がこの国の観光に来ています。

   (　　　　) and (　　　　) people are coming for sightseeing in this country.
2. その店ではさまざまな種類の野菜を買うことができます。

   You can buy a (　　　　) (　　　　) vegetables at the store.
3. 寒くて，そのうえ，風も強かった。

   It was cold, and (　　　　) (　　　　), it was windy.

D　Arrange the words in the proper order to match the Japanese.

【知識・技能（表現・文法）】（各4点）

1. あなたは昼食にサンドイッチを持っていきたいですか。

   Do you (sandwiches / take / to / want / with / you) for lunch?

   ....

2. 私はあなたがそのトーナメントに勝ったと知って驚いた。

   I was surprised (know / that / the tournament / to / won / you).

   ....

3. 彼女はその音楽に魅了された人の1人です。

   She is (by / fascinated / of / one / that music / the people).

   ....

E　Fill in each blank with a suitable word from the passage.

【思考力・判断力・表現力（内容）】（各5点）

1. A French man is (　　　　) to a young couple in his Japanese lunchbox shop.
2. Many foreign people are (　　　　) by Japanese bento culture.
3. The Japanese bento is beautiful and (　　　　).

11

Part 3   教科書 p.29

A   Write the English words to match the Japanese.   【知識・技能（語彙）】（各2点）

1. .... 形 独特の B1
2. .... 形 オランダの
3. .... 名 紙箱, カートン B1
4. .... 名 ピーナッツ B1
5. .... 名 ゼリー A2
6. .... 名 容器 A2

B   Choose the word whose underlined part's sound is different from the other three.

【知識・技能（発音）】（各2点）

1. ア. <u>ch</u>ildren   イ. <u>Ch</u>inese   ウ. <u>Ch</u>ristmas   エ. Dut<u>ch</u>
2. ア. am<u>o</u>ng   イ. c<u>o</u>ver   ウ. l<u>o</u>ve   エ. p<u>o</u>pular
3. ア. althou<u>gh</u>   イ. dau<u>gh</u>ter   ウ. enou<u>gh</u>   エ. thou<u>gh</u>t

C   Complete the following English sentences to match the Japanese.

【知識・技能（表現・文法）】（完答・各3点）

1. 紙といっしょにペンも持ってきてください。

   Please bring some paper, (　　　　) (　　　　) pens.

2. 私たちはきれいな落ち葉でおおわれた道を散歩しました。

   We took a walk in the road (　　　　) (　　　　) beautiful fallen leaves.

3. 今日遅刻しました。それは寝坊したからです。

   I was late for school today. This is (　　　　) I overslept this morning.

D   Arrange the words in the proper order to match the Japanese.

【知識・技能（表現・文法）】（各4点）

1. コアラやカンガルーのような動物はオーストラリア特有だ。

   Animals such as koalas and kangaroos (are / Australia / to / unique).

   ----

2. 親が子供のために料理をするのが一般的です。

   It is (common / cook / for / parents / to) for their children.

   ----

3. その歌は世界中の人々に長い間人気がある。

   That music (among / around the world / been / has / people / popular) for a long time.

E   Fill in each blank with a suitable word from the passage.

【思考力・判断力・表現力（内容）】（各5点）

1. Dutch people prepare lunches of (　　　　) ham or cheese sandwiches.
2. American people put sandwiches, fruit, a small (　　　　) of juice, and sometimes snacks into a lunchbox.
3. Chinese people use (　　　　) to carry bentos.

Part 4 　教科書 p.32 　　　／52

A Write the English words to match the Japanese. 【知識・技能（語彙）】（各 2 点）

1. .... 形 自家製の B1 　　2. .... 形 バランスの取れた B1

3. .... 形 楽しい，魅力的な A2 　4. .... 副 きちんと，適切に B1

5. .... 图 効用，機能 A2

B Choose the word whose stressed syllable is different from the other three.

【知識・技能（発音）】（各 2 点）

1. ア．com-mon 　　イ．func-tion 　　ウ．sand-wich 　　エ．u-nique

2. ア．ar-range 　　イ．con-tain 　　ウ．daugh-ter 　　エ．re-ceive

3. ア．at-trac-tive 　　イ．pop-u-lar 　　ウ．prop-er-ly 　　エ．typ-i-cal

C Complete the following English sentences to match the Japanese.

【知識・技能（表現・文法）】（完答・各 3 点）

1. 彼は自信に満ちあふれている。

   He is (　　　　) (　　　　) confidence.

2. 彼は最も嫌いな科目さえも勉強することができた。

   He was able to study (　　　　) his (　　　　) favorite subjects.

3. 冷たいものを飲みすぎることは健康を損なうことがある。

   Having too much cold drink may (　　　　) (　　　　) unhealthy.

D Arrange the words in the proper order to match the Japanese.

【知識・技能（表現・文法）】（各 4 点）

1. Lesson 1 の学習は終わりました。

   (finished / have / of / the study / we) Lesson 1.

   ----

2. そのすばらしいニュースは日本中の人々を幸せな気持ちにしました。

   That wonderful (happy / in / Japan / made / news / people).

   ----

3. その母親は子供に一生懸命勉強するように促した。

   That mother (encouraged / hard / her children / study / to).

E Fill in each blank with a suitable word from the passage.

【思考力・判断力・表現力（内容）】（各 5 点）

1. Japanese parents always think about their children (　　　　) they are making bentos.

2. *Kyaraben* are created from parents' (　　　　).

3. Japanese-style bentos can be a remarkable (　　　　) tool.

Activity Plus 教科書 p.36〜p.37 　/54

A Write the English words to match the Japanese. 【知識・技能（語彙）】（各2点）

1. _____ 图 ちらし，リーフレット B2 　2. _____ 图 テーマ，主題 B2
3. _____ 副 地元で 　4. _____ 图 登録 B1
5. _____ 動 …を提出する B2 　6. _____ 動 …を仕上げる B1

B Choose the word whose stressed syllable is different from the other three.

【知識・技能（発音）】（各2点）

1. ア．com-plete 　イ．con-test（名詞） 　ウ．coun-try 　エ．en-try
2. ア．en-ter 　イ．pro-duce（動詞） 　ウ．sub-mit 　エ．u-nique
3. ア．en-cour-age 　イ．fas-ci-nate 　ウ．lo-cal-ly 　エ．prop-er-ly

C Complete the following English sentences to match the Japanese.

【知識・技能（表現・文法）】（完答・各3点）

1. 弁当が好きです。理由が2つあります。1つは美しいということともう1つは健康によいということです。

   I like bentos.　I have two reasons.　One is because they are beautiful, and
   (　　　) (　　　) is because they are healthy.

2. この用紙に記入して，事務所に提出してください。

   Please (　　　) out this form and (　　　) it to the office.

3. ボーイフレンドに靴を探しています。

   I am looking for a (　　　) (　　　) shoes for my boyfriend.

D Arrange the words in the proper order to match the Japanese.

【知識・技能（表現・文法）】（各4点）

1. 彼らはあなたが会議に参加することを望んでいる。

   They hope (in / part / take / that / will / you) the meeting.

   _____

2. 今年の文化祭のテーマは何ですか。

   (is / of / our school festival / the theme / what) this year?

   _____

3. あそこでフルートを吹いている女の子は私の友達です。

   The girl (is / my friend / over there / playing / the flute).

   _____

E Fill in each blank with a suitable word from the passage.

【思考力・判断力・表現力（内容）】（各5点）

1. If you win International Bento Contest, you can get a pair of round-trip (　　　) to Hokkaido.

2. Entry period for the contest is from (　　　) 25 to May 6, 2025.

3. If you are (　　　) than 14 years old, you can join the contest.

総合問題

/50

Read the following passage and answer the questions below.

"Do you (A)(with / to / want / take / miso soup / you) for lunch? Do you use a microwave?" A French man is talking to a young couple in his Japanese lunchbox shop in Kyoto. He is one of the many foreign people (B)fascinate by Japanese bento culture. He is selling Japanese lunchboxes to travelers in the shop. He is (C)(also / to / people / selling / them / abroad) through the Internet.

Many people in other countries are surprised to know that the Japanese bento is beautiful. In a typical bento, a variety of bite-sized foods are neatly arranged (1) a lunchbox. It is very colorful and looks like a (2) of art. More and more people want to try making this art.

(3), the bento is healthy. It usually contains many foods, like rice, meat, fish, vegetables and fruit. It is a full-course meal in a small box.

1. 空所(1), (2), (3)に入る適切な語を選びなさい。　　　　　【知識・技能（語彙・表現）】(各4点)

  (1) ア. for　　　　イ. from　　　　ウ. into　　　　エ. with
  (2) ア. cook　　　イ. food　　　　ウ. variety　　　エ. work
  (3) ア. Finally　　イ. For example　ウ. In addition　エ. Therefore

2. 下線部(A), (C)の（　　）内の語句を適切に並べかえなさい。　　　【知識・技能（文法）】(各5点)

  (A) ....
  (C) ....

3. 下線部(B) fascinate を適切な形に変えなさい。　　　　　　　　【知識・技能（文法）】(4点)

  (　　　　　　　　　)

4. 本文の内容に合っているものをすべて選びなさい。　　　【思考力・判断力・表現力（内容）】(完答・8点)

  ア. A French man is selling microwaves in Kyoto.
  イ. The young couple bought a Japanese-style bentos in Japan.
  ウ. Many foreigners are surprised to know that the Japanese bento is beautiful.
  エ. In a typical Japanese bento, a variety of bite-sized foods are used.
  オ. The Japanese bento contains only main dish, like meat and fish.

5. 次の問いの答えになるよう，空所に適切な語を補いなさい。

　　　　　　　　　　　　　　　　　　　　　　　　【思考力・判断力・表現力（内容）】(完答・各8点)

  (1) What is the French man fascinated by?
    —— He is fascinated by (　　　　) (　　　　) (　　　　).
  (2) Why do many people want to try making Japanese bento?
    —— Because it is (　　　　) and (　　　　).

15

ディクテーション

Listen to the English and write down what you hear.

Part 1

You found a Q&A site about the Japanese bento.

I'm planning to travel to Japan next week and want to try some bentos. Any (1.　　　　)? Lilly

You should visit a Japanese convenience store. Each store has a large section for bentos, and you can choose one from a wide (2.　　　　). You can see some typical Japanese foods, such as sushi, noodles and curry. Victor

You should try *ekiben*, or "station bentos." You can buy them at stations for long-distance trains. Buy your bento before (3.　　　　) and enjoy it on the train. At some stations, you can buy popular local bentos, such as a *gyutan* bento at Sendai Station. Emily

If you stay in a big city like Tokyo or Osaka, you should go to a (4.　　　　) area on your lunch break. A lot of restaurants sell bentos to business people. They are made by a restaurant chef, but they are not so (5.　　　　). David

Part 2

The Japanese bento is growing popular overseas. Many non-Japanese are enjoying making and eating bentos. Why are they interested in this Japanese-style box lunch?

1　"Do you want to take miso soup with you for lunch? Do you use a (1.　　　　)?" A French man is talking to a young couple in his Japanese (2.　　　　) shop in Kyoto. He is one of the many foreign people (3.　　　　) by Japanese bento culture. He is selling Japanese lunchboxes to travelers in the shop. He is also selling them to people (4.　　　　) through the Internet.

2　Many people in other countries are (5.　　　　) to know that the Japanese bento is beautiful. In a (6.　　　　) bento, a variety of bite-sized foods are neatly arranged into a lunchbox. It is very colorful and looks like a work of art. More and more people want to try making this art.

3　In addition, the bento is healthy. It usually (7.　　　　) many foods, like rice, meat, fish, vegetables and fruit. It is a full-course meal in a small box.

Part 3

4　The idea of (1.　　　　) bentos to school or work is not (2.　　　　) to Japan.

5　(3.　　　　) people prepare lunches of simple ham or cheese sandwiches, along with some fruit, like an apple or a banana. They make sandwiches for themselves, and it is not common to prepare them for someone else.

6　(4.　　　　) people put sandwiches, fruit, a small carton of juice, and sometimes snacks into a lunchbox. There are a variety of sandwiches, but peanut butter and jelly sandwiches have been popular among (5.　　　　　) for a long time.

⑦ The Chinese-style box lunch contains rice covered with one or two main dishes, such as stir-fried (6.　　　　). Chinese people use containers to carry bentos, and they always warm the box lunch up before they eat it. This is because they don't like to eat (7.　　　　) food.

Part 4

⑧ Japanese (1.　　　　) bentos are full of love. In Japan, many high school students eat a bento made by their parents for lunch. The parents get up early in the morning and make their bentos. "Will my son like these side dishes?" "Is this bento well-balanced for my (2.　　　　)?" They always think about such things while they are making bentos.

⑨ *Kyaraben*, or "(3.　　　　) bentos," are created from parents' love. They want to make the food (4.　　　　) and encourage their kids to eat properly. Their kids are able to eat even their (5.　　　　) favorite foods.

⑩ Japanese parents put (6.　　　　) into the bentos, and the children receive them. Some people in other countries have noticed this function of bentos, and they also enjoy making them. Japanese-style bentos can be a remarkable (7.　　　　) tool around the world.

Activity Plus

You are interested in joining a bento contest. You are looking at a leaflet about it.

International Bento Contest (1.　　　　)

The White Snow Bento Company has held an International Bento Contest since (2.　　　　). The 10th contest will start on April 25, 2025. The theme this year is "a bento using locally-produced foods." The first-prize winner will get a pair of round-trip (3.　　　　) to Hokkaido from his/her country. We hope that you will take part in this contest!

Contest Rules

Entry Period: From April 25 to May 6, 2025

Theme: A bento (4.　　　　) locally-produced foods

How to Enter: Fill out the entry form, and submit your recipe and pictures through the contest website.

Take two pictures. One should be a picture of all foods before cooking, and the other should be a picture of the (5.　　　　) bento.

Entry Conditions: You must be 15 or older to join the contest.

For more information, visit our (6.　　　　) at https://www.wsbc.com/2025/contest/

Part 1　教科書 p.42〜p.43　　/46

A　Write the English words to match the Japanese.　【知識・技能（語彙）】（各2点）

1. .... 图 人口 A2　　　　2. .... 動 減少する B1

B　Choose the word whose underlined part's sound is different from the other three.

【知識・技能（発音）】（各2点）

1. ア．face　　　　イ．graph　　　ウ．hand　　　エ．photo
2. ア．Japan　　　イ．number　　ウ．public　　エ．young
3. ア．call　　　　イ．local　　　ウ．phone　　エ．total

C　Complete the following English sentences to match the Japanese.

【知識・技能（表現・文法）】（完答・各3点）

1. グラフからわかるように，最近ではテレビを観る人は少ない。

（　　　）（　　　）can（　　　）in the graph, less people watch TV these days.
2. 一方で，この5年間で，タブレットを使用する人の数は増えた。

（　　　）（　　　）（　　　）（　　　）, the number of tablet users has（　　　）in the last five years.
3. タブレットの導入により紙の使用量は10％減少した。

The use of paper has（　　　）（　　　）10% thanks to the introduction of tablets.

D　Arrange the words in the proper order to match the Japanese.

【知識・技能（表現・文法）】（各4点）

1. タブレットで新聞を読むことは，20年前にはそれほど一般的でなかった。

Reading newspapers (a tablet / common / not / on / very / was) 20 years ago.

----
2. 年々，タブレットの使用は増え続けていくだろう。

The use of tablets (by / continue / increase / to / will / year / year).

----
3. このことは，将来，紙の新聞を読む人が少なくなることを意味する。

(less / means / people / read / that / this / will) paper newspapers in the future.

E　Fill in each blank with a suitable word from the passage.

【思考力・判断力・表現力（内容）】（完答・各5点）

1. The graph shows the changes in the total numbers of（　　　）and（　　　）（　　　）in Japan.
2. In 2011, there were more than（　　　）（　　　）cellphones.
3. From 1990 to 2017, the number of（　　　）（　　　）decreased by more than 80%.

Part 2　教科書 p.44　　/54

A Write the English words to match the Japanese.　　【知識・技能（語彙）】（各2点）

1. ....　图 発展，進化 B2　　2. ....　動 発展する B2
3. ....　動 重さが…ある A2　　4. ....　图 バッテリー，電池 A2
5. ....　形 手のひらに乗る　　6. ....　形 持ち運びできる,携帯用の

B Choose the word whose underlined part's sound is different from the other three.

【知識・技能（発音）】（各2点）

1. ア．b<u>oa</u>t　　イ．<u>e</u>volve　　ウ．h<u>o</u>me　　エ．m<u>o</u>st
2. ア．b<u>a</u>ck　　イ．b<u>a</u>ttery　　ウ．h<u>a</u>ppen　　エ．v<u>a</u>rious
3. ア．call<u>ed</u>　　イ．develop<u>ed</u>　　ウ．evolv<u>ed</u>　　エ．happen<u>ed</u>

C Complete the following English sentences to match the Japanese.

【知識・技能（表現・文法）】（完答・各3点）

1. 釣りのこととなると，リエは私のクラスでだれよりも詳しい。

（　　　　）it（　　　　）（　　　　）fishing, nobody knows more than Rie in my class.
2. 最近では，海釣りをする女性が多い。

（　　　　）, there are many women（　　　　）go fishing in the sea.
3. 女性用の釣りウェアはこの数年で進化してきた。

Ladies' fishing wear（　　　　）（　　　　）over the past few years.

D Arrange the words in the proper order to match the Japanese.

【知識・技能（表現・文法）】（各4点）

1. これはリエが先月釣った魚の写真だ。

This is the photo (caught / last month / of / Rie / the fish / which).

----

2. その魚は体長60センチあり，約4キロの重さだった。

The fish was (about / and / four kilograms / long / weighed / 60 centimeters).

----

3. 昨夜リサは友人に国際電話をかけた。

Lisa (an / call / made / overseas / phone / to) her friend last night.

E Fill in each blank with a suitable word from the passage.

【思考力・判断力・表現力（内容）】（各5点）

1. Dr. Martin Cooper was an (　　　　) at a telecommunications company in the U.S.
2. The first cellphone was (　　　　) by him.
3. The battery of the first cellphone (　　　　) only 20 minutes.

19

Part 3　教科書 p.45　　/54

A　Write the English words to match the Japanese.　【知識・技能（語彙）】（各2点）

1. _____ 图 おまけ，余分なもの A2　　2. _____ 图 機能，特徴 A2

3. _____ 图 道具 B1　　4. _____ 图 アプリケーション B1

5. _____ 图 ツールボックス,道具箱　　6. _____ 图 解決策 A2

B　Choose the word whose underlined part's sound is different from the other three.

【知識・技能（発音）】（各2点）

1. ア．feature　　イ．instead　　ウ．release　　エ．screen

2. ア．add　　イ．draw　　ウ．talk　　エ．wall

3. ア．butter　　イ．function　　ウ．solution　　エ．subject

C　Complete the following English sentences to match the Japanese.

【知識・技能（表現・文法）】（完答・各3点）

1. 当時の日本には車はなかった。

There were no cars in Japan (　　　　) (　　　　) (　　　　).

2. オンラインショッピングサイトのおかげで，私たちは家で物を買うことができる。

(　　　　) (　　　　) the online shopping sites, we can buy things at home.

3. 彼は今年を新しい人生の始まりと考えている。

He thinks (　　　　) this year (　　　　) a beginning of his new life.

D　Arrange the words in the proper order to match the Japanese.

【知識・技能（表現・文法）】（各4点）

1. そのスーツケースはとても重くて，私には運べなかった。

The suitcase was (carry / could not / heavy / I / it / so / that).

----

2. コンピュータ・プログラミングを学ぶのは，私には簡単ではなかった。

It (easy / for / learn / me / not / to / was) computer programming.

----

3. 止まらずに25メートル泳げたので，私は水泳が好きになった。

I (because / came / I / like / swimming / to / was able to) swim 25 meters without

stopping.

E　Fill in each blank with a suitable word from the passage.

【思考力・判断力・表現力（内容）】（各5点）

1. The first cellphone for public use was (　　　　) on the market in 1983.

2. In 2000, a camera function was (　　　　) to cellphones.

3. The (　　　　) of the images was low, so people at that time thought of it as an

extra.

Part 4　教科書 p.48

A Write the English words to match the Japanese.　【知識・技能（語彙）】（各2点）

1. .... 副 いつかは, ついに B1　　2. .... 副 急速に B1

3. .... 图 10年間 B2　　4. .... 图 外見 A2

5. .... 副 技術的に　　6. .... 動 …を助ける B1

B Choose the word whose stressed syllable is different from the other three.

【知識・技能（発音）】（各2点）

1. ア. ap-pear-ance　　イ. bad-min-ton　　ウ. com-pa-ny　　エ. li-brar-y

2. ア. en-gi-neer　　イ. in-tro-duce　　ウ. Jap-a-nese　　エ. mu-si-cian

3. ア. beau-ti-ful-ly　　イ. Jan-u-ar-y　　ウ. tech-nol-o-gy　　エ. tel-e-vi-sion

C Complete the following English sentences to match the Japanese.

【知識・技能（表現・文法）】（完答・各3点）

1. グリーンエネルギーが将来, エネルギー市場を席巻するだろう。

   Green energy will (　　　　) (　　　　) the energy market in the future.

2. 彼は人生でひどい時期を経験した。

   He (　　　　) (　　　　) a bad time in his life.

3. 私の弟はまったくテレビゲームをしない。

   My younger brother does not play video games (　　　　) (　　　　).

D Arrange the words in the proper order to match the Japanese.

【知識・技能（表現・文法）】（各4点）

1. 私たちはここで約100年間ずっとブドウを育てています。

   We (been / for / grapes / growing / have / here) about one hundred years.

   ----

2. 彼のチームが優勝すると期待されている。

   It (expected / his team / is / that / will / win) the championship.

   ----

3. 二次元コードはその製品をユーザーマニュアルと結び付ける。

   The QR code (its user manual / link / the product / to / will).

E Fill in each blank with a suitable word from the passage.

【思考力・判断力・表現力（内容）】（各5点）

1. The cellphone has been (　　　　) rapidly in the past ten years.

2. People need more functions on their cellphones, and companies are trying to (　　　　) their needs.

3. In the near future, cellphones will not have a (　　　　) screen.

Activity Plus 　教科書 p.52〜p.53

/49

A　Write the English words to match the Japanese.　【知識・技能（語彙）】（各 2 点）

1. .... 图 接触 A2
2. .... 图 レンズ
3. .... 形 ふつうの A2
4. .... 副 自動的に A2
5. .... 動 …を結合させる B1
6. .... 動 …を操作する A2

B　Choose the word whose stressed syllable is different from the other three.

【知識・技能（発音）】（各 2 点）

1. ア．con-tact　　　イ．cor-rect　　　ウ．en-joy　　　エ．ex-pect
2. ア．ex-hi-bi-tion　イ．in-ter-est-ed　ウ．math-e-mat-ics　エ．pre-sen-ta-tion
3. ア．au-to-mat-i-cal-ly　　　　　　イ．en-vi-ron-men-tal-ly
　　ウ．in-ter-na-tion-al-ly　　　　　エ．tech-no-log-i-cal-ly

C　Complete the following English sentences to match the Japanese.

【知識・技能（表現・文法）】（完答・各 3 点）

1. プレゼンテーションをすることは，ディスカッションのよい練習になる。

　　(　　　　) (　　　　) (　　　　　) is a good practice for a discussion.

2. 必要ならば，計算機を使えます。

　　When it (　　　　) (　　　　), you can use a calculator.

3. カナダにいたとき，あなたの家族の一員になったように感じました。

　　When I was in Canada, I felt I was (　　　　) (　　　　) your family.

D　Arrange the words in the proper order to match the Japanese.

【知識・技能（表現・文法）】（各 4 点）

1. その寺の正面に大きな桜の木がある。

　　There (a large cherry tree / front / in / is / of / the temple).

　　---

2. その有名玩具メーカーは新しいおもちゃを『フラッフィエッグ』と名付けた。

　　(famous / *Fluffy Egg* / named / their new toy / the / toymaker).

　　---

3. 今日は新商品のアイディアについてお話しします。

　　Today, (about / going / I'm / my idea / tell / to / you) for a new product.

E　Fill in each blank with a suitable word from the passage.

【思考力・判断力・表現力（内容）】（完答・各 5 点）

1. You can (　　　　) a special lens in your eye like a normal contact lens. Then, the lens can catch your brain (　　　　).

2. The Wi-Fi hub (　　　　) to the Internet.

総合問題

/50

Read the following passage and answer the questions below.

　The first cellphone for public use was released on the market in 1983.　It was only for talking.　Its screen was so (A)(it / that / use / easy / to / not / the cellphone / small / was).　Since then, telecommunications companies have put their efforts into adding other functions, along (　1　) the talking function.

　In 2000, a camera function was added (　2　) cellphones.　The quality of the images was low, so people at that time thought of (B)it as an extra.　Then, "the wallet cellphone" was introduced in 2004.　Thanks to (C)it, people could buy things with their cellphones. (　3　) various features were added, screens became bigger and cellphones became easier to use.　People came (D)(of / to / devices / use / instead / cellphones / other), such as dictionaries and music players.

　Cellphones are not just for talking anymore.　They are portable devices.　Companies have developed various applications and have changed cellphones into toolboxes with a solution for almost every need.

1.　空所(1), (2), (3)に入る適切な語を選びなさい。　【知識・技能（語彙・表現）】（各4点）

　(1)　ア．by　　　　　イ．for　　　　　ウ．to　　　　　エ．with

　(2)　ア．from　　　　イ．of　　　　　ウ．to　　　　　エ．up

　(3)　ア．Although　　イ．As　　　　　ウ．But　　　　　エ．Or

2.　下線部(A), (D)の（　　）内の語句を適切に並べかえなさい。　【知識・技能（文法）】（各4点）

　(A) ....

　(D) ....

3.　下線部(B), (C)が指す具体的な内容を本文中から抜き出しなさい。【思考力・判断力・表現力（内容）】（各4点）

　(B) ....　　(C) ....

4.　本文の内容に合っているものをすべて選びなさい。　【思考力・判断力・表現力（内容）】（完答・10点）

　ア．The first public phone was released in 1983.

　イ．People were able to take photos with their cellphones in the 1990s.

　ウ．Some people used cellphones to look up the meanings of words.

　エ．People now carry toolboxes with them anywhere.

5.　次の問いの答えになるよう，空所に適切な語を補いなさい。【思考力・判断力・表現力（内容）】（完答・各6点）

　(1)　What have telecommunications companies done since the first cellphone for public use was released on the market?

　　── They have put their (　　　　　) into adding other functions and have developed various (　　　　) for cellphones.

　(2)　What have cellphones been changed into?

　　── They have been changed into (　　　　　) with a solution for almost every (　　　　).

23

ディクテーション

Listen to the English and write down what you hear.

Part 1

You want to learn some information about cellphones and public phones. You are listening to a presentation about them.

The total numbers of cellphones and public phones in Japan from 1990 to 2017

　The (1.　　　) shows the changes in the total numbers of cellphones and public phones in Japan from 1990 to 2017.

　As you can see, before 1993, cellphones were not very (2.　　　). From 1999 to 2008, the total number of cellphones (3.　　　) by more than 100%. In 2011, there were more than 120 million cellphones. This means that the number of cellphones was greater than the (4.　　　) of Japan. Even today, the number is increasing year by year.

　On the other hand, from 1990 to 2017, the number of public phones (5.　　　) by more than 80%. Will the number of public phones continue to decrease year by year?

Part 2

Can you live without your cellphone? Most people use their cellphones for various purposes. The evolution of the cellphone over the last 50 years is an amazing story.

① A lot of things have happened in the last 50 years. When it comes to (1.　　　), "50 years ago" is like ancient times. What has evolved surprisingly fast as technology has developed? Yes, it's the (2.　　　).

② Nowadays, seven billion cellphones are used around the world. Who (3.　　　) the cellphone? It was Dr. Martin Cooper, an (4.　　　) at a telecommunications company in the U.S.

③ Cooper invented the first cellphone in 1973. He wanted to make a phone which people could carry with them (5.　　　). The first model was 22.5 centimeters long and weighed about one kilogram. The battery (6.　　　) only 20 minutes.

④ In 1973, Cooper stood on a street in New York and made a phone (7.　　　). He said, "I'm calling from a cellphone! A real handheld, portable cellphone!"

Part 3

⑤ The first cellphone for (1.　　　) use was released on the market in 1983. It was only for talking. Its screen was so small that it was not easy to use the cellphone. Since then, telecommunications companies have put their efforts into adding other (2.　　　), along with the talking function.

⑥ In 2000, a camera function was added to cellphones. The quality of the images was low, so people at that time thought of it as an (3.   ). Then, "the wallet cellphone" was introduced in 2004. Thanks to it, people could buy things with their cellphones. As various features were added, (4.   ) became bigger and cellphones became easier to use. People came to use cellphones instead of other (5.   ), such as dictionaries and music players.

7 Cellphones are not just for talking anymore. They are (6.   ) devices. Companies have developed various applications and have changed cellphones into toolboxes with a (7.   ) for almost every need.

Part 4

8 (1.   ) were introduced in 2007. Today, most people have a smartphone. Some people expect that smartphones will eventually take over the cellphone market.

9 The cellphone has been evolving rapidly in the past (2.   ). Both its appearance and purpose have changed during that time. People need more (3.   ) on their cellphones, and companies are trying to meet their needs. The evolution of the cellphone is an important event in the history of telecommunications technology.

10 In the future, cellphones will go through another big change. It is expected that we will not need a (4.   ) screen at all in the near future. It is thought that we will be able to link the devices to our brain and control them with our (5.   ). This will be a technologically-assisted form of telepathy.

11 What do you think the future phone will look like? You may (6.   ), "How will we change the cellphone?" The real question is, "How will the cellphone change us?"

Activity Plus

Koji and Airi are making a presentation about their ideas for a future phone.
"A Special Contact Lens"

Hi. I'm Koji. My idea for a future phone is a (1.   ) type of phone. I named it "A Special Contact Lens."

You can wear a lens in your eye like a (2.   ) contact lens. The lens can catch your brain waves. When it is necessary, a screen automatically appears in the air. Only the user can see it. The phone (3.   ) several computers through the Internet. You can operate it with your thoughts.

"New Face: Part of My Fashion"

Hi. I'm Airi. Today, I'm going to tell you about my idea for a future phone. I call it "New Face." It's (4.   ) of my fashion.

The phone is an earring and a bracelet. The earring shows the screen in front of you. The bracelet is a Wi-Fi hub. It connects to the Internet.

It's a (5.   ) future phone!

Part 1 　教科書 p.58〜p.59 　　/54

A　Write the English words to match the Japanese. 　【知識・技能（語彙）】（各2点）

1. _____ 名 アナウンス・放送文 B1　2. _____ 名 生息地 B1

3. _____ 動 …のように見える A2　4. _____ 名 基金 B1

5. _____ 形 絶滅の危機に瀕した A2　6. _____ 名 （生物の）種 B2

B　Choose the word whose underlined part's sound is different from the other three.

【知識・技能（発音）】（各2点）

1.　ア. <u>c</u>age 　　　イ. <u>c</u>entimeter 　　ウ. <u>c</u>limb 　　　エ. <u>c</u>oat

2.　ア. announ<u>c</u>ement 　イ. len<u>s</u> 　　　ウ. <u>s</u>eem 　　　エ. <u>s</u>ymbol

3.　ア. end<u>a</u>ngered 　イ. h<u>a</u>bitat 　　ウ. kilo<u>ca</u>lorie 　　エ. p<u>a</u>nda

C　Complete the following English sentences to match the Japanese.

【知識・技能（表現・文法）】（完答・各3点）

1.　彼には10年以上会っていない。

　　I haven't seen him for (　　　　) (　　　　) ten years.

2.　ベスは演奏を上達させるために毎日ピアノを練習した。

　　Beth practiced the piano every day (　　　　) (　　　　) (　　　　) improve her

　　performance.

3.　私たちは泣かないようにしたが，泣かずにはいられなかった。

　　We (　　　　) (　　　　) (　　　　) cry, but we couldn't help it.

D　Arrange the words in the proper order to match the Japanese.【知識・技能（表現・文法）】（各4点）

1.　オーストラリアは日本の約20倍の大きさだ。

　　Australia is (about / of / the size / times / twenty) Japan.

　　--

2.　昨日，国中の多くの人たちがそのニュースを聞いて驚いた。

　　Yesterday, (a lot / all / of / over / people / the country) were surprised to hear the

　　news.

　　--

3.　あのネコは高い木の上手な登り方を知っているようだ。

　　That cat (climb / how / know / seems / to / to) tall trees well.

　　--

E　Fill in each blank with a suitable word from the passage.【思考力・判断力・表現力（内容）】（各5点）

1.　The (　　　　) of giant pandas is about 1,800 in the wild.

2.　Pandas first came to Ueno Zoo as a symbol of the (　　　　) between China and

　　Japan.

3.　Since the foundation of World Wide Fund for Nature, the number of pandas has

　　(　　　　) little by little.

26

A Write the English words to match the Japanese.　【知識・技能（語彙）】（各 2 点）

1. .... 图 気候 B1
2. .... 图 生存 B1
3. .... 图 連合 B1
4. .... 图 保護 B1
5. .... 图 絶滅 B1
6. .... 图 生態系 B1

B Choose the word whose underlined part's sound is different from the other three.

【知識・技能（発音）】（各 2 点）

1. ア. addition　　イ. announcement　ウ. change　　エ. climate
2. ア. each　　イ. head　　ウ. healthy　　エ. threaten
3. ア. fund　　イ. future　　ウ. human　　エ. union

C Complete the following English sentences to match the Japanese.

【知識・技能（表現・文法）】（完答・各 3 点）

1. ダニエルと私は多くの共通点を持っていたので，よい友達になった。

   Daniel and I had many things (　　　) (　　　), so we became good friends.
2. 天気予報によると，今日は快晴になるとのことだ。

   (　　　) (　　　) the weather report, it will be clear today.
3. 学校の購買部ではマスクが売られるべきだ。

   Masks should (　　　) (　　　) at the school store.

D Arrange the words in the proper order to match the Japanese.

【知識・技能（表現・文法）】（各 4 点）

1. 彼女はピアノに加えてギターを練習し始めた。

   She began to (addition / in / practice / the guitar / the piano / to).

2. この NGO は，地域の自然環境を保護することにおいて中心的な役割を果たしている。

   This NGO has been (a / central / in / playing / role) protecting the natural environment of the area.

3. この箱は，中に花瓶が入っているので丁寧に取り扱われる必要がある。

   This box (be / care / handled / should / with) because it has a vase in it.

E Fill in each blank with a suitable word from the passage.

【思考力・判断力・表現力（内容）】（各 5 点）

1. Pandas, polar bears and gorillas are all (　　　) animals.
2. The International Union for the Conservation of Nature is working to save species from (　　　).
3. All animals are necessary for the (　　　) of nature.

Part 3 　教科書 p.62　　　　/52

A　Write the English words to match the Japanese.　【知識・技能（語彙）】（各2点）

1. .... 動 …を寄付する B2　　2. .... 動 傾向がある B1

3. .... 名 宣伝，広告 A2　　4. .... 名 保護 B1

5. .... 名 好み B1

B　Choose the word whose stressed syllable is different from the other three.

【知識・技能（発音）】（各2点）

1. ア．do-nate　　イ．liz-ard　　ウ．on-ly　　エ．per-cent

2. ア．at-trac-tive　　イ．do-na-tion　　ウ．en-dan-gered　　エ．pref-er-ence

3. ア．how-ev-er　　イ．per-son-al　　ウ．pol-lu-tion　　エ．pro-tec-tion

C　Complete the following English sentences to match the Japanese.

【知識・技能（表現・文法）】（完答・各3点）

1. 彼はその慈善団体に多額の寄付をした。

   He (　　　) (　　　) large (　　　) to the charity.

2. 幼い子供は大人に比べてかぜをひきやすい。

   Small children (　　　) (　　　) catch more colds than adults.

3. 個人的な好みは，時に私たちの意思決定に影響を与えるようだ。

   (　　　) (　　　) that our personal preferences sometimes affect our decision-making.

D　Arrange the words in the proper order to match the Japanese.【知識・技能（表現・文法）】（各4点）

1. 先生は生徒たちに，自分の町の好きな場所について話すように言った。

   The teacher told his students to talk about (in / liked / places / that / they) their towns.

   ....

2. その問題はまだ解決されていないようだ。

   (hasn't / it / seems / that / the problem) been solved yet.

   ....

3. 北海道への旅行を計画されているというのは本当ですか。

   (are / is / it / that / true / you) planning a trip to Hokkaido?

   ....

E　Fill in each blank with a suitable word from the passage.【思考力・判断力・表現力（内容）】（各5点）

1. In the survey, almost all the people answered that they would be interested in (　　　).

2. According to the survey, almost half of the people would donate for the endangered animals that they (　　　).

3. Some companies tend to use animals that people find attractive or cute in (　　　).

Part 4　教科書 p.63　　/54

A Write the English words to match the Japanese.　【知識・技能（語彙）】（各2点）

1. .... 名 特徴 B1
2. .... 動 …を無視する B1
3. .... 動 …を得る B1
4. .... 名 利益 B1
5. .... 形 農業の B1
6. .... 名 調和 A2

B Choose the word whose stressed syllable is different from the other three.

【知識・技能（発音）】（各2点）

1. ア. for-get　　イ. ig-nore　　ウ. in-sect　　エ. our-selves
2. ア. ben-e-fit　　イ. fam-i-ly　　ウ. foun-da-tion　　エ. har-mo-ny
3. ア. ag-ri-cul-tur-al　イ. char-ac-ter-is-tic　ウ. in-ter-na-tion-al　エ. pos-si-bil-i-ty

C Complete the following English sentences to match the Japanese.

【知識・技能（表現・文法）】（完答・各3点）

1. このアプリには2つの長所がある。第一にはたくさんの情報が入っていて，第二には使いやすい。

   This app has two merits. (　　　　), it has a lot of information, and (　　　　), it is easy to use.

2. 残念ながら，このメッセージは無視されるだろう。

   Unfortunately, this message will (　　　　) (　　　　).

3. サラとメアリーは互いに調和しながら歌っていた。

   Sarah and Mary were singing (　　　　) (　　　　) (　　　　) each other.

D Arrange the words in the proper order to match the Japanese.

【知識・技能（表現・文法）】（各4点）

1. 毎朝ジョギングをするのは，私にはよいことだと思いますか。

   Do you think (for / go / good / is / it / me / to) jogging every morning?

2. 私たちは，人間が自然の一部であることを忘れがちである。

   We tend (are / forget / human beings / part / that / to) of nature.

3. 彼女は英語だけではなく，スペイン語も勉強している。

   She studies (also / but / English / not / only / Spanish).

E Fill in each blank with a suitable word from the passage.

【思考力・判断力・表現力（内容）】（各5点）

1. Some people say that (　　　　) today is for "beautiful and useful species only."
2. Benefits we gain from the natural environment are called ecosystem (　　　　).
3. By protecting the environment and endangered species, we help both the endangered animals and (　　　　).

29

Activity Plus

教科書 p.68〜p.69

/54

A Write the English words to match the Japanese. 【知識・技能（語彙）】（各2点）

1. ＿＿＿＿＿＿＿ 形 絶滅した B1　　2. ＿＿＿＿＿＿＿ 名 意識 B1
3. ＿＿＿＿＿＿＿ 動 貢献する B1　　4. ＿＿＿＿＿＿＿ 動 …を観測する B1
5. ＿＿＿＿＿＿＿ 動 …を保存する, 守る B1　6. ＿＿＿＿＿＿＿ 名 連鎖, 鎖 A2

B Choose the word whose underlined part's sound is different from the other three.

【知識・技能（発音）】（各2点）

1. ア．Ar<u>c</u>tic　　イ．<u>c</u>limate　　ウ．<u>c</u>ontribute　　エ．i<u>c</u>e
2. ア．d<u>o</u>nation　　イ．m<u>o</u>nitor　　ウ．<u>o</u>cean　　エ．p<u>o</u>lar
3. ア．camp<u>aig</u>n　　イ．ch<u>ai</u>n　　ウ．f<u>ai</u>r　　エ．r<u>ai</u>se

C Complete the following English sentences to match the Japanese.

【知識・技能（表現・文法）】（完答・各3点）

1. もし大きな地震がこの地域を襲うと，私たちの家は危険にさらされるだろう。

   If a big earthquake hits this area, our house will (　　　　) (　　　　) (　　　　).

2. その会社は，新製品に対する認識を高めるために，広告を発表した。

   The company released an advertisement to (　　　　) (　　　　) of their new product.

3. きみはぼくたちの勝利に貢献してくれた。だからきみをとても誇りに思うよ。

   You have (　　　　) (　　　　) our victory, so I'm very proud of you.

D Arrange the words in the proper order to match the Japanese.

【知識・技能（表現・文法）】（各4点）

1. 忙しい日程のせいで，私はその約束をキャンセルしなければならなかった。

   I (because / cancel / had / of / the appointment / to) my busy schedule.

   ＿＿＿＿＿＿＿＿＿＿＿＿＿＿＿＿＿＿＿＿＿＿

2. ここは騒々しいです。静かな部屋をお願いできますか。

   It is noisy here. (a / ask / could / for / I / quiet / room)?

   ＿＿＿＿＿＿＿＿＿＿＿＿＿＿＿＿＿＿＿＿＿＿

3. この話し合いではどんな考えでも歓迎します。

   In this meeting, (any / be / ideas / welcomed / will).

   ＿＿＿＿＿＿＿＿＿＿＿＿＿＿＿＿＿＿＿＿＿＿

E Fill in each blank with a suitable word from the passage.

【思考力・判断力・表現力（内容）】（各5点）

1. Polar bears spend most of their lives on the sea ice of the (　　　　) Ocean.
2. Polar bears may become (　　　　) in the near future.
3. Help Polar Bears has started a five-year (　　　　).

総合問題

/50

Read the following passage and answer the questions below.

　There is an interesting survey. One thousand people were asked to donate some money for endangered animals. Almost all the people answered that they would be interested in donating. What kinds of animals did they want to make a donation to help?

　According (　1　) the survey, 43 percent of the people would donate for the endangered animals that they liked, such as pandas and koalas. On the other hand, they would not (A)(animals / didn't / donate / for / like / they), such as snakes and lizards. Most of them answered that it was not fair to help only attractive animals, though.

　(　2　) seems that people like to protect animals that they find attractive or cute. Some companies (B)(animals / in / such / tend / to / use) advertisements to raise their sales. It is true that we are making efforts to protect endangered animals. (　3　), the animals that receive our protection are often decided by our personal preferences.

　Why do we think that bears and pandas are cute? First, they have human-like characteristics. Second, they live in a family setting, like bears and their babies. (　4　), we like larger animals. Most smaller species, such as insects, tend to be ignored. Some people say that conservation today is for "beautiful and useful species only."

1.　空所(1), (2), (3)に入る適切な語を選びなさい。　　　　【知識・技能（語彙・表現）】（各4点）

(1)　ア．for　　　　　　イ．in　　　　　　　ウ．of　　　　　　　エ．to

(2)　ア．It　　　　　　　イ．That　　　　　ウ．They　　　　　エ．This

(3)　ア．Also　　　　　イ．First　　　　　ウ．However　　　エ．So

2.　空所(4)に適切な語を補いなさい。　　　　　　　　　　　【知識・技能（語彙・表現）】（4点）

（　　　　　　　）

3.　下線部(A), (B)の（　　）内の語句を適切に並べかえなさい。　【知識・技能（文法）】（各4点）

(A)　--

(B)　--

4.　本文の内容に合っているものをすべて選びなさい。　【思考力・判断力・表現力（内容）】（完答・10点）

ア．In the survey, many people were interested in donating for endangered animals.

イ．Most of the people answered that only attractive animals should be helped.

ウ．We often decide the animals for protection with our personal preferences.

エ．Most smaller species live in a family setting.

オ．We should conserve only beautiful and useful species.

5.　次の問いの答えになるよう，空所に適切な語を補いなさい。【思考力・判断力・表現力（内容）】（完答・各8点）

(1)　How many people were asked to donate some money for endangered animals?

　　―（　　　　　　）（　　　　　　）people were.

(2)　What do bears and pandas have?

　　― They have（　　　　　）（　　　　　）.

ディクテーション

Listen to the English and write down what you hear.

Part 1

You are visiting a zoo. You see giant pandas and find a notice in front of their cage. Also, you hear an announcement about pandas.

Giant Pandas

Height: Adults can grow to more than 120 centimeters

Weight: 100-150 kilograms

A baby panda is about 1/900 the size of its mother.

Population: About 1,800 in the wild (about 400 in zoos)

Habitat: Bamboo forests in China

Pandas first came to Ueno Zoo from China in 1972 as a ($_1$.　　) of the friendship between China and Japan. A lot of people went to see them at the zoo. In 1994, a panda came to Wakayama. There is a ($_2$.　　) base there for giant pandas. More than ten pandas have been born there. Pandas are very ($_3$.　　) all over Japan.

This animal with a black and white ($_4$.　　) is loved around the world. Pandas live mainly in bamboo forests in China. They must eat from 10 to 40 kilograms of bamboo every day, and they need 4,000 kilocalories a day to stay ($_5$.　　). In order to save energy, they try not to move much. They seem to move very slowly, but pandas are very good at ($_6$.　　) trees.

The panda is special for World Wide Fund for Nature, or WWF. It has been WWF's symbol since its ($_7$.　　) in 1961. Since then, the number of pandas has increased little by little. They are symbols of all ($_8$.　　) species.

Part 2

Almost everyone likes to see pandas. But how about snakes? Are they necessary for our planet, or not?

1　What do pandas, polar bears and gorillas have in ($_1$.　　)? Yes, they are all animals. In addition to being animals, they are all endangered animals. They might ($_2$.　　) in the near future. Climate change, pollution and human activities are ($_3$.　　) their survival.

2　The International Union for the Conservation of Nature, or IUCN, is working to ($_4$.　　) species from extinction. The IUCN Red List of Threatened Species is used to guide decision-making for ($_5$.　　) action. According to the list, more than 13,000 animal species are threatened with extinction.

3　We all care about saving species from extinction, but a question might come to mind: "Why should endangered species be ($_6$.　　)?" It is because all species play a role in nature. All species of life on earth are ($_7$.　　) to each other and are needed for our planet to stay healthy. All animals are part of the global ecosystem and are necessary for the ($_8$.　　) of nature.

Part 3

④ There is an interesting (1.   ). One thousand people were asked to donate some money for endangered animals. Almost all the people answered that they would be (2.   ) in donating. What kinds of animals did they want to make a donation to help?

⑤ According to the survey, 43 percent of the people would donate for the endangered animals that they (3.   ), such as pandas and koalas. On the other hand, they would not donate for animals they didn't like, such as snakes and lizards. Most of them answered that it was not fair to help only (4.   ) animals, though.

⑥ It seems that people like to protect animals that they find attractive or cute. Some companies tend to use such animals in (5.   ) to raise their sales. It is true that we are making efforts to protect endangered animals. However, the animals that (6.   ) our protection are often decided by our personal (7.   ).

Part 4

⑦ Why do we think that bears and pandas are (1.   )? First, they have human-like characteristics. Second, they live in a family (2.   ), like bears and their babies. Lastly, we like larger animals. Most smaller species, such as insects, tend to be ignored. Some people say that (3.   ) today is for "beautiful and useful species only." Is it good for us to protect only those species?

⑧ We should not forget that human beings are one of the species on earth. Human society is part of the global (4.   ). We gain a lot of benefits from the natural environment and from the ecosystem. They are called ecosystem services. They are the (5.   ) of all food and agricultural systems.

⑨ Our lives are closely connected to ecosystem services. By protecting the environment and endangered species, we help not only the endangered animals but also (6.   ). We have to think about this: "How can we live in (7.   ) with nature on a healthy planet?"

Activity Plus

You are looking at a poster about saving polar bears.
Save the Polar Bear!

Do you know that polar bears spend most of their lives on the sea (1.   ) of the Arctic Ocean? They hunt for food and raise their (2.   ) on the ice.

Due to climate change, the sea ice is (3.   ). Because of this, polar bears may become extinct in the near future. Their future is in great danger.

Help Polar Bears, an NGO, wants to protect polar bears. It has started a five-year campaign to raise (4.   ) about their situation. We ask for your support. Any donations will be welcomed. The money will contribute to the following five areas:

  1. Tracking polar bear mothers   2. Monitoring polar bear habitats
  3. (5.   ) future polar bear habitats   4. Understanding climate change
  5. Preserving the Arctic food chain

You can help polar bears and their polar home by supporting Help Polar Bears. We need your help. If you are interested in this (6.   ), please contact us at https://www.helppolarbears.com.

Part 1　教科書 p.74〜p.77

/50

A　Write the English words to match the Japanese.　【知識・技能（語彙）】（各 2 点）

1. ....　图 展示（品）　2. ....　图 好奇心 B1

3. ....　動 …を含む A2　4. ....　形 記録資料による, ドキュメンタリーの

B　Choose the word whose stressed syllable is different from the other three.

【知識・技能（発音）】（各 2 点）

1. ア. chil-dren　　　イ. cul-ture　　　ウ. e-vent　　　エ. sci-ence

2. ア. ad-ven-ture　　イ. ap-pear-ance　ウ. cu-ri-ous　　エ. ex-hib-it

3. ア. char-ac-ter-is-tic　イ. cu-ri-os-i-ty　ウ. doc-u-men-ta-ry　エ. in-ter-na-tion-al

C　Complete the following English sentences to match the Japanese.

【知識・技能（表現・文法）】（完答・各 3 点）

1. 彼は好奇心をもって教科書を読んでいる。

   He is reading his textbook (　　　　) (　　　　).

2. 将来彼の性格が彼を困らせることになるでしょう。

   His character will get him (　　　　) (　　　　) in the future.

3. 彼女が突然現れたので, 私は驚いた。

   Her sudden (　　　　) surprised me.

D　Arrange the words in the proper order to match the Japanese.

【知識・技能（表現・文法）】（各 4 点）

1. 彼は私の誕生日にすてきなプレゼントをくれた。

   He (a / gave / me / present / wonderful) for my birthday.

   ----

2. あなたの努力により, あなたはよい選手になれるでしょう。

   Your effort (a good player / become / lead / to / will / you).

   ----

3. その犬はあなたを危険から救った。

   That dog (danger / helped / of / out / you).

E　Fill in each blank with a suitable word from the passage.

【思考力・判断力・表現力（内容）】（各 5 点）

1. You can experience a lot of new things with (　　　　).

2. You can see special appearance by George, (　　　　) with one of his stories.

3. All tickets (　　　　) one special documentary movie.

Part 2 教科書 p.78

A Write the English words to match the Japanese. 【知識・技能（語彙）】（各2点）

1. .... 图 創作者 B1
2. .... 形 ユダヤ人の
3. .... 形 一生の B1
4. .... 動 …と結婚する A2
5. .... 動 …を出版する A2
6. .... 图 出版社，発行者 B1

B Choose the word whose underlined part's sound is different from the other three.

【知識・技能（発音）】（各2点）

1. ア. h<u>u</u>man   イ. c<u>u</u>te   ウ. f<u>u</u>ture   エ. p<u>u</u>blish
2. ア. cr<u>ea</u>tor   イ. <u>e</u>scape   ウ. m<u>a</u>rry   エ. pl<u>a</u>ce
3. ア. c<u>ou</u>ntry   イ. en<u>ou</u>gh   ウ. s<u>ou</u>th   エ. t<u>ou</u>ch

C Complete the following English sentences to match the Japanese.

【知識・技能（表現・文法）】（完答・各3点）

1. 先生は私にレポートのタイトルを変更させた。

The teacher (   ) me (   ) the title of my report.
2. ジョンが引っ越してからしばらくの間，連絡がない。

John and I have lost (   ) for a (   ) since he moved out.
3. 私たちはオーストラリアで出会ったとき，お互いに恋に落ちました。

We (   ) (   ) love with each other when we met in Australia.

D Arrange the words in the proper order to match the Japanese.

【知識・技能（表現・文法）】（各4点）

1. 私は彼のために絵を描く機会があった。

I (a chance / a picture / had / paint / to) for him.

----
2. 彼らは9月に結婚し，その後ずっと幸せに暮らした。

(got / in / married / they) September and lived happily ever after.

----
3. 母は私に部屋の掃除をさせた。

(clean / made / me / my mother / my room).

E Fill in each blank with a suitable word from the passage.

【思考力・判断力・表現力（内容）】（各5点）

1. Hans Augusto Rey developed a lifelong love for (   ) and drawing.
2. Margret was a young (   ) girl.
3. Hans and Margret traveled to Paris and decided to (   ) there.

Part 3   教科書 p.79   /54

A   Write the English words to match the Japanese.   【知識・技能（語彙）】（各2点）

1. .... 名 軍隊，陸軍 B1   2. .... 動 …に近づく B2

3. .... 形 予備の B2   4. .... 形 利用[入手]できる B1

5. .... 名 原稿   6. .... 名 難民，避難民 B2

B   Choose the word whose stressed syllable is different from the other three.

【知識・技能（発音）】（各2点）

1. ア．ap-proach   イ．ar-my   ウ．Jew-ish   エ．mil-lion

2. ア．man-u-script   イ．pub-lish-er   ウ．rap-id-ly   エ．ref-u-gee

3. ア．an-i-ma-tion   イ．a-vail-a-ble   ウ．ex-pe-ri-ence   エ．po-lit-i-cal

C   Complete the following English sentences to match the Japanese.

【知識・技能（表現・文法）】（完答・各3点）

1. 彼は両親に会うために出発した。

   He (   ) (   ) to meet his parents.

2. 第二次世界大戦が勃発したとき，私の祖父母は危険にさらされていた。

   When World War II (   ) out, my grandparents were in (   ).

3. ほんの数か月前に，私はテニスを始めた。

   Only (   ) (   ) months ago, I started to play tennis.

D   Arrange the words in the proper order to match the Japanese.

【知識・技能（表現・文法）】（各4点）

1. 彼らはクマから逃げる方法を見つけなければならなかった。

   They (a way / away / find / had / run / to / to) from the bear.

   ----

2. 今日ご利用できるバスの運行はありません。

   There (are / available / bus / no / services) today.

   ----

3. 彼はその問題を避けようとしている。

   He (away / from / get / is trying / the problem / to).

E   Fill in each blank with a suitable word from the passage.

【思考力・判断力・表現力（内容）】（各5点）

1. World War II started in 1939, shortly after Hans' book was (   ).

2. In June 1940, the Nazi (   ) was rapidly approaching Paris.

3. On June 12, 1940, the Reys left Paris on their (   ) with the manuscript of *Fifi: The Adventures of a Monkey*.

Part 4   教科書 p.80

/54

A Write the English words to match the Japanese. 【知識・技能（語彙）】（各2点）

1. .... 图 小屋，家畜小屋 B2   2. .... 形 疑い深い B2
3. .... 图 なまり，アクセント B1 4. .... 形 いたずら好きな
5. .... 動 …を反映する A2   6. .... 形 無邪気な，無知な B1

B Choose the word whose underlined part's sound is different from the other three.

【知識・技能（発音）】（各2点）

1. ア. deci̲de   イ. i̲nnocent   ウ. mi̲schief   エ. suspici̲ous
2. ア. a̲ccent   イ. cha̲racter   ウ. da̲nger   エ. pa̲ssion
3. ア. behi̲nd   イ. hi̲storic   ウ. smi̲le   エ. sp̲y

C Complete the following English sentences to match the Japanese.

【知識・技能（表現・文法）】（完答・各3点）

1. 学校から家に帰る途中に，彼女に偶然出会った。

   I happened to see her (   ) the (   ) home from school.

2. 今日の授業で学んだ内容を復習しておきなさい。

   Review (   ) you (   ) in today's lesson.

3. 私は彼がその試験に合格すると確信している。

   I am (   ) (   ) he would pass the exam.

D Arrange the words in the proper order to match the Japanese.

【知識・技能（表現・文法）】（各4点）

1. 彼らがこの状態から抜け出すことは難しい。

   It is difficult (for / it / make / out of / them / to) this situation.

   ----

2. 買う必要があるもののリストを作っておきなさい。

   Keep (a list / buy / need / of / to / what / you).

   ----

3. 彼女はその見かけから裕福なように思える。

   She (be / from / her appearance / rich / seems / to).

E Fill in each blank with a suitable word from the passage.

【思考力・判断力・表現力（内容）】（各5点）

1. The checkpoint officer became (   ) of the Reys' German accents.
2. Their cute little (   ) helped the Reys pass through Spain and made it out of Europe.
3. A historic (   ) was behind a warm character of innocent mischief.

Activity Plus 　教科書 p.84〜p.85　　/50

A　Write the English words to match the Japanese.　【知識・技能（語彙）】（各 2 点）

1. _____ 名（映画の）監督 A2　　　2. _____ 名 情熱 B1

3. _____ 名 映画制作　　　　　　　4. _____ 動 …を感激させる B1

B　Choose the word whose underlined part's sound is different from the other three.

【知識・技能（発音）】（各 2 点）

1. ア. director　　　イ. docum<u>e</u>ntary　　　ウ. experience　　　エ. together

2. ア. creator　　　イ. escape　　　ウ. passion　　　エ. safely

3. ア. Brazil　　　イ. film　　　ウ. history　　　エ. inspire

C　Complete the following English sentences to match the Japanese.

【知識・技能（表現・文法）】（完答・各 3 点）

1. 彼がトーナメントに勝ったことを知って私は刺激を受けた。

I (　　　) (　　　) when I knew that he won the tournament.

2. その情報はみんなと共有したほうがいいよ。

That information should (　　　) (　　　) with everyone.

3. このクラスのみんなは彼をリーダーだとみなしている。

Everyone in this class (　　　) him (　　　) a leader.

D　Arrange the words in the proper order to match the Japanese.

【知識・技能（表現・文法）】（各 4 点）

1. なぜあなたは数学の先生になることを決断したのですか。

(become / decide / made / to / what / you) a math teacher?

2. 本への情熱が私を小説家の職へと導いた。

(books / for / led / me / the passion / to) the job of novelist.

3. 電車の中に傘を置いてきてしまった。

I (behind / left / my umbrella / on / the train).

E　Fill in each blank with a suitable word from the passage.

【思考力・判断力・表現力（内容）】（各 5 点）

1. Ema Ryan Yamazaki decided to study (　　　) in college and it has led her to her career today.

2. She loved *Curious George*, and happened to learn about the (　　　) of it.

3. She hopes our (　　　) will drive us to discover what we like.

総合問題

/50

Read the following passage and answer the questions below.

Only a few months after Hans' book was published, World War II broke out in 1939. (1) they were German Jews in Paris, Hans and Margret Rey felt they would be in danger. (2) June 1940, the Nazi army was rapidly approaching Paris.

There were no more trains, and the Reys didn't own a car. They (A)(a way / away / from / had / to find / to get) Paris. Hans hurried over to a bicycle shop, but there were no bicycles for them. Only spare parts were available. That night, Hans (B)(make / put / the parts / to / together / two bicycles).

Early in the morning of June 12, 1940, the Reys (3) off on their bicycles. They took very little with them: warm clothes, some food and some unpublished manuscripts of children's books. They included one special book, *Fifi: The Adventures of a Monkey*. It was just 48 hours before the Nazi army marched into Paris. They were finally among the millions of refugees (C)try to run away to the south.

1. 空所(1), (2), (3)に入る適切な語を選びなさい。　　　【知識・技能（語彙・表現）】（各4点）

(1)　ア．After　　　　イ．Before　　　　ウ．Since　　　　エ．Though

(2)　ア．At　　　　　イ．During　　　　ウ．In　　　　　エ．On

(3)　ア．got　　　　　イ．made　　　　　ウ．put　　　　　エ．set

2. 下線部(A), (B)の（　　）内の語句を適切に並べかえなさい。　【知識・技能（文法）】（各4点）

(A) --

(B) --

3. 下線部(C) try を適切な形に変えなさい。　　　　　　　　【知識・技能（文法）】（4点）

(　　　　　　　)

4. 本文の内容に合っているものをすべて選びなさい。　　【思考力・判断力・表現力（内容）】（完答・10点）

ア．World War II broke out before Hans' book was published.

イ．Only Hans felt that he would be in danger.

ウ．When Hans went to a bicycle shop, there were no bicycles for them.

エ．In June 1940, the Nazi army was rapidly approaching Paris.

オ．The Reys couldn't get out of Paris because they had some unpublished manuscripts.

5. 次の問いの答えになるよう，空所に適切な語を補いなさい。

【思考力・判断力・表現力（内容）】（完答・各8点）

(1)　Why did the Reys had to use bicycles?

―― Because there were no more (　　　　　) and they didn't own a (　　　　　).

(2)　How long did it take for the Nazi army to march into Paris after the Reys left?

―― It took only (　　　　　) hours.

ディクテーション

Listen to the English and write down what you hear.

Part 1

You want to go to a *Curious George* exhibit with your family. You are looking at the exhibit website.

Museum of Culture and Science

Special (1.   ) Events

Let's Have Fun with *Curious George*!

　Do you know a cute little monkey that always gets himself into (2.   )? Yes, it's George, Curious George! He is a good little monkey and always very curious.

　This (3.   ) leads him to meet a man with a yellow hat and to travel from Africa to get a new home in a zoo. His curiosity gets George into trouble, but it always helps him out of it.

　Let's (4.   ) the world of *Curious George*! In these exhibit events, you can see buildings and places from the *Curious George* books and (5.   ). Experience a lot of new things with curiosity. These special events will give you a wonderful experience you won't forget!

　Special appearance by George, along with one of his stories, at 10 a.m. and 1 p.m.!

TICKETS

・$21 for adults from 13 to 64　　・$19 for adults 65 and over

・$16 for children from 2 to 12 (Children under 2 are free.)

　A ticket includes one special 45-minute (6.   ) movie.

TIME

・Monday through Saturday from 10 a.m. to 5 p.m.　　・Sunday from noon to 6 p.m.

PLACE

　Museum of Culture and Science

　401 North Second Street, Green Forest, FL 333XX

Part 2

While millions of people know *Curious George*, not many people know about the careers of his creators. How did they create one of the world's most famous monkeys?

① Hans Augusto Rey was born in Germany in 1898 to Jewish (1.   ). He grew up a few blocks from a zoo. So he developed a lifelong love for animals and (2.   ). He met a young Jewish girl, Margret, at her sister's birthday party. Later, Margret left her hometown to study art, and they lost (3.   ) for a while.

② In 1935, Hans and Margret met again in Brazil. Hans was doing some family (4.   ). Margret was escaping the political climate in Germany. They decided to start working together. They soon fell in love and got (5.   ) in August.

③ In 1936, Hans and Margret traveled to Paris, France. They enjoyed Paris so much that they decided to stay there. Then Hans had a chance to (6.   ) some of his animal drawings in a French magazine. His drawings became quite (7.   ). That made the publisher decide to publish Hans' first children's book, *Raffy and the Nine Monkeys*, in 1939.

Part 3

4 Only a few months after Hans' book was published, World War II (1.   ) out in 1939. Since they were German Jews in Paris, Hans and Margret Rey felt they would be in (2.   ). In June 1940, the Nazi army was rapidly approaching Paris.

5 There were no more trains, and the Reys didn't own a car. They had to find a way to get away from Paris. Hans (3.   ) over to a bicycle shop, but there were no bicycles for them. Only spare parts were (4.   ). That night, Hans put the parts together to make two bicycles.

6 Early in the morning of June 12, 1940, the Reys (5.   ) off on their bicycles. They took very little with them: warm clothes, some food and some unpublished (6.   ) of children's books. They included one special book, *Fifi: The Adventures of a Monkey*. It was just 48 hours before the Nazi army marched into Paris. They were finally among the millions of (7.   ) trying to run away to the south.

Part 4

7 Hans and Margret slept in (1.   ) and on floors of restaurants on the way south. Finally, they came across running trains. This was their chance to get out of France. However, a checkpoint officer became (2.   ) of their German accents. When he (3.   ) their bags and found the manuscript of *Fifi*, he was sure that they were not German spies. Thanks to their cute little (4.   ), the Reys passed through Spain and made it out of Europe to Brazil by ship. After reaching Brazil, they continued on to New York.

8 In October 1940, Hans and Margret arrived safely in America. One year later, *Fifi: The Adventures of a Monkey* was published in America (5.   ) the new name: *Curious George*.

9 Think of all the smiles around the world that have been made by one (6.   ) little monkey! *Curious George* seems to reflect what his creators experienced while they were escaping the Nazis. Who knew such a historic adventure was behind a warm character of (7.   ) mischief?

Activity Plus

In 2017, the *Curious George* documentary *MONKEY BUSINESS* was released by a film director, Ema Ryan Yamazaki. You are listening to an interview with her.

Q1) What made you decide to become a film (1.   )?

When I was in high school, I began telling stories with a camera. I realized I had a passion for sharing what I found interesting with others. So I decided to study filmmaking in college, and it has led me to this (2.   ).

Q2) Why did you choose *Curious George* and its creators as the theme of your work?

I happened to learn about the (3.   ) of *Curious George* from a friend. I loved *Curious George*, but I didn't know anything about his creators before then. I was inspired when I knew that they experienced hardships but left behind wonderful stories and a cute character. I thought that their story should be (4.   ) with the world.

Q3) Please give your message to high school students.

I was (5.   ) to find my passion in high school, and now I have a career in doing what I enjoy the most. I learned a lot from the creators of *Curious George*. I hope your curiosity will drive you to discover what you like and to see life as an (6.   ).

Part 1 　教科書 p.90～p.91　　/54

A　Write the English words to match the Japanese.　【知識・技能（語彙）】（各2点）

1. ＿＿＿＿＿＿ 图 給料 B2　　　　2. ＿＿＿＿＿＿ 形 公務の, 公式の A2

3. ＿＿＿＿＿＿ 图 官邸, 住宅, 邸宅 B2　4. ＿＿＿＿＿＿ 图 経済 B1

5. ＿＿＿＿＿＿ 動 抗議する B2　　　6. ＿＿＿＿＿＿ 動 …を逮捕する B1

B　Choose the word whose underlined part's sound is different from the other three.

【知識・技能（発音）】（各2点）

1. ア．angry　　イ．animal　　ウ．date　　　エ．salary

2. ア．condition　イ．life　　　ウ．official　　エ．simple

3. ア．arrest　　イ．protest　　ウ．residence　エ．theme

C　Complete the following English sentences to match the Japanese.

【知識・技能（表現・文法）】（完答・各3点）

1. 彼は生まれ故郷で静かな生活を過ごした。

He (　　　　) a (　　　　) (　　　　) in his hometown.

2. 彼女は大統領官邸に引っ越す予定である。

She is going to move to the president's (　　　　) (　　　　).

3. 彼女の家族は, 彼女の少ない収入で暮らしていた。

Her family (　　　　) (　　　　) her small income.

D　Arrange the words in the proper order to match the Japanese.

【知識・技能（表現・文法）】（各4点）

1. 私が留守の間, ネコの世話をしてくれませんか。

Can (care / cats / my / of / take / while / you) I'm away?

2. そのクラシックカーは良好な状態だった。

The (a / car / classic / condition / good / in / was).

3. 彼は大学を卒業した後, 海外へ行くことを決心した。

He decided (abroad / after / from / go / graduated / he / to) university.

E　Fill in each blank with a suitable word from the passage.

【思考力・判断力・表現力（内容）】（各5点）

1. Mujica lives near Montevideo, the (　　　　) of Uruguay.

2. He was released in 1985 and became a (　　　　) ten years later.

3. In 2009, he was elected (　　　　) of Uruguay.

Part 2 教科書 p.92

/54

A Write the English words to match the Japanese. 【知識・技能（語彙）】（各2点）

1. _____ 動 ぶら下がる，つるしてある B1
2. _____ 形 毎月の B1
3. _____ 图 収入 B1
4. _____ 图 義務 B1
5. _____ 形 民間人の，国家の B1
6. _____ 图 大多数 B1

B Choose the word whose underlined part's sound is different from the other three.

【知識・技能（発音）】（各2点）

1. ア．c<u>a</u>lm   イ．l<u>au</u>ndry   ウ．l<u>aw</u>   エ．t<u>a</u>ll
2. ア．po<u>ll</u>ution   イ．d<u>u</u>ty   ウ．f<u>u</u>ll   エ．sol<u>u</u>tion
3. ア．elect<u>ed</u>   イ．research<u>ed</u>   ウ．watch<u>ed</u>   エ．work<u>ed</u>

C Complete the following English sentences to match the Japanese.

【知識・技能（表現・文法）】（完答・各3点）

1. この劇は日本の民話に由来する。
   This play (　　　　) (　　　　) a Japanese folktale.
2. その警官は通りでスリを見張った。
   The police officer (　　　　) (　　　　) for pickpockets on the street.
3. この部屋は私の子供時代の思い出でいっぱいです。
   This room is (　　　　) (　　　　) memories in my childhood.

D Arrange the words in the proper order to match the Japanese.

【知識・技能（表現・文法）】（各4点）

1. 研究者たちはそのフルーツについて新しい研究を実施した。
   The (a / carried / new / on / out / researchers / study) the fruit.

   _____

2. 前アメリカ大統領が先週，日本を訪れた。
   The (former / Japan / of / president / the United States / visited) last week.

   _____

3. 生徒会長に選ばれた生徒を知っていますか。
   Do you (elected / know / president / the student / was / who) of the student council?

   _____

E Fill in each blank with a suitable word from the passage.

【思考力・判断力・表現力（内容）】（各5点）

1. When he was a president, Mujica (　　　　) most of his salary to charities.
2. He was seen as "the (　　　　) president in the world."
3. He thinks a president should be a civil (　　　　).

Part 3 教科書 p.93

/54

A Write the English words to match the Japanese.　【知識・技能（語彙）】（各2点）

1. ＿＿＿＿＿＿＿＿ 形 普段着の, カジュアルな B1　　2. ＿＿＿＿＿＿＿＿ 動 (意見)を述べる, …を届ける B2

3. ＿＿＿＿＿＿＿＿ 名 貧困 B1　　4. ＿＿＿＿＿＿＿＿ 動 …を強調する B2

5. ＿＿＿＿＿＿＿＿ 名 孤独 B2　　6. ＿＿＿＿＿＿＿＿ 名 財産, 富 A2

B Choose the word whose underlined part's sound is different from the other three.

【知識・技能（発音）】（各2点）

1. ア．clothes　　イ．loneliness　　ウ．most　　エ．poverty

2. ア．casual　　イ．police　　ウ．residence　　エ．stress

3. ア．friend　　イ．leader　　ウ．president　　エ．wealth

C Complete the following English sentences to match the Japanese.

【知識・技能（表現・文法）】（完答・各3点）

1. 私は生まれて初めて雪を見た。

   I saw the snow (　　　　) the (　　　　) (　　　　) in my life.

2. 英語でスピーチをすることは私には難しい。

   (　　　) (　　　) (　　　) in English is difficult for me.

3. 教室に入ると, もう授業は始まっていた。

   When I entered the classroom, the class (　　　) already (　　　).

D Arrange the words in the proper order to match the Japanese.

【知識・技能（表現・文法）】（各4点）

1. このウールのセーターを着ていると温かい。

   I (feel / in / this / warm / wool / sweater).

   ----

2. 結婚したとき, 15年間私たちは知り合いであった。

   When we got married, (each / for / had / known / other / we / 15 years).

   ----

3. 持っているもので1週間生活しなければならなかった。

   I (I / had / had to / live / what / with) for a week.

E Fill in each blank with a suitable word from the passage.

【思考力・判断力・表現力（内容）】（各5点）

1. When Mujica was invited to Japan, a Japanese (　　　　) had just begun to sell the book about him.

2. He said, "If people cannot share the feeling of (　　　　) with their family, friends or neighbors, they are poor."

3. According to him, the poorest person is the one who (　　　　) a lot to live.

Part 4 　教科書 p.94

/54

A Write the English words to match the Japanese. 【知識・技能（語彙）】（各2点）

1. .... 動 …を教育する B1　2. .... 形 物欲的な，物質的な
3. .... 图 消費者 B1　4. .... 動 …を追い求める，追う A2
5. .... 图 成長 B1　6. .... 形 満足している B1

B Choose the word whose stressed syllable is different from the other three.

【知識・技能（発音）】（各2点）

1. ア．ec-o-nom-ic　　イ．es-pe-cial-ly　　ウ．ma-te-ri-al　　エ．po-lit-i-cal
2. ア．ed-u-ca-tion　　　　　　　　イ．pol-i-ti-cian
   ウ．tem-per-a-ture　　　　　　　エ．un-der-stand-ing
3. ア．in-dus-tri-al-ize　イ．o-rig-i-nal-ly　ウ．un-com-fort-a-ble　エ．u-ni-ver-si-ty

C Complete the following English sentences to match the Japanese.

【知識・技能（表現・文法）】（完答・各3点）

1. 外国を訪れるたびに，私は美しい絵葉書を妹に送る。

   (　　　　) (　　　　) I visit a foreign country, I send a beautiful postcard to my sister.
2. よいリーダーは常に一人一人の意見を尊重する。

   A good leader always (　　　　) (　　　　) of each person's opinion.
3. どこで試験を受けるか，インターネットで見ることができます。

   You can see (　　　　) you will take the examination on the Internet.

D Arrange the words in the proper order to match the Japanese.

【知識・技能（表現・文法）】（各4点）

1. ネコにいつえさをやるべきかを教えてくれませんか。

   Can you (the cats / feed / I / me / should / tell / when)?

   ----
2. 彼はいつも自由時間は映画を観て過ごす。

   He (his / always / movies / spends / time / watching / free).

   ----
3. その医者は彼女の生命を心配していない。

   (about / does / her / life / not / the doctor / worry).

E Fill in each blank with a suitable word from the passage.

【思考力・判断力・表現力（内容）】（完答・各5点）

1. Mujica said that Japanese students should ask themselves (　　　　) happiness is and (　　　　) poverty is.
2. He told them that (　　　　) is not what matters most.
3. He stressed that life is not only about (　　　　) money.

45

Activity Plus 　教科書 p.98〜p.99　　/54

A　Write the English words to match the Japanese.　　【知識・技能（語彙）】（各2点）

1. _____ 图 データ，資料，情報 B2　2. _____ 前 …につき B1
3. _____ 图 予想値　　　　　　　4. _____ 動 …を評価する A2
5. _____ 图 福祉 B2　　　　　　　6. _____ 前 …に関しては B1

B　Choose the word whose stressed syllable is different from the other three.

【知識・技能（発音）】（各2点）

1. ア．Den-mark　　　イ．Eu-rope　　　ウ．Ja-pan　　　　エ．Nor-way
2. ア．hap-pi-ness　　イ．i-mag-ine　　　ウ．im-por-tant　　エ．re-gard-ing
3. ア．e-con-o-my　　イ．en-vi-ron-ment　ウ．Eu-ro-pe-an　　エ．tech-nol-o-gy

C　Complete the following English sentences to match the Japanese.

【知識・技能（表現・文法）】（完答・各3点）

1. 以下は日報の一例である。
   (　　　　) (　　　　) is an example of our daily report.
2. 日本はある意味では豊かな国の一つだ。
   Japan is one of the rich countries (　　　) (　　　) (　　　).
3. 彼の家族は1か月につき1,000ドルで生活する。
   His family lives on 1,000 dollars (　　　) (　　　).

D　Arrange the words in the proper order to match the Japanese.

【知識・技能（表現・文法）】（各4点）

1. その質問は，お客様に満足度を評価するよう求めている。
   The question (asks / rate / the customers / their satisfaction / to).

   ----

2. その新プログラムにつきましては，当社カスタマーサービスにご連絡ください。
   Please (contact / customer / our / regarding / service / the new program).

   ----

3. この報告書では，世界の国々が人口によって順位付けされている。
   In this report, (are / by / countries / of / ranked / the population / the world).

E　Fill in each blank with a suitable word from the passage.

【思考力・判断力・表現力（内容）】（完答・各5点）

1. According to the World Happiness Report, (　　　　) (　　　　) countries rank in the top five each year.
2. On the other hand, Japan ranks much (　　　　) in the report.
3. Japan is the (　　　　) among the G7 nations.

総合問題

/50

Read the following passage and answer the questions below.

Mujica thinks highly of (A)educate young people. (　1　) a politician, he believes that good education has the power to change the world in the future.　Every time he visits a foreign country, he gives a speech to young people, especially university students.

In Tokyo, Mujica said that Japanese students should (B)(and / ask / happiness is / poverty is / themselves / what / what).　He told them that wealth is not what matters most, and that we should not spend all of our time worrying (　2　) material things. He stressed that life is not only about earning money.　(C)His words greatly impressed the young people of Japan.

Japan is a highly developed country, and we are surrounded (　3　) various kinds of consumer goods and high-tech products.　Japan has pursued economic growth (　4　) decades, but many people say they are not (D)satisfy.　A survey shows that people's sense of happiness in Japan is not very high among the (E)industrialize nations.　Jose Mujica's message teaches us very important things about (F)(about / happiness / how / should / think / we).

1.　空所(1), (2), (3), (4)に入る適切な語を語群から選んで書きなさい。【知識・技能（語彙・表現）】（各2点）

(1) (　　　　　)　　(2) (　　　　　)　　(3) (　　　　　)　　(4) (　　　　　)

〔 about, as, by, for, in, to 〕

2.　下線部(A), (D), (E)の語を適切な形に変えなさい。　　　　　　【知識・技能（文法）】（各2点）

(A) (　　　　　)　　(D) (　　　　　)　　(E) (　　　　　)

3.　下線部(B), (F)の (　　) 内の語句を適切に並べかえなさい。　【知識・技能（文法）】（各4点）

(B) ....

(F) ....

4.　下線部(C)の文の主語を The young people of Japan にして書きかえなさい。

【知識・技能（文法）】（4点）

The young people of Japan ....

5.　本文の内容に合っているものをすべて選びなさい。　【思考力・判断力・表現力（内容）】（完答・10点）

ア．Mujica told the students that wealth is the most important thing.

イ．People get stressed when their lives don't go well.

ウ．Japan is one of the developing countries.

エ．Our lives in Japan are full of consumer goods and high-tech products.

6.　次の問いの答えになるよう，空所に適切な語を補いなさい。【思考力・判断力・表現力（内容）】（完答・各7点）

(1)　What does Mujica do when he visits a foreign country?

　　── He gives a (　　　　　) to young people.

(2)　What did Mujica stress in his speech in Tokyo?

　　── He stressed that (　　　　　) is not only about earning money.

ディクテーション

Listen to the English and write down what you hear.

Part 1

You are listening to a poster presentation about "The Poorest President in the World."
The Poorest President in the World

Jose Mujica   Born: May 20, 1935

Family: wife, pets and other animals   His Life —— Very Unusual for a President!

Mr. Mujica …

· leads a very (1.   ) life near Montevideo, the capital of Uruguay.

· loves taking care of animals and plants on his farm.

· likes reading very much and gives most of his books to schools later.

· never wears expensive clothes and never wears a tie, even with his suit.

· lived on a (2.   ) salary even when he was the president.

· didn't live in the president's official (3.   ), and didn't use the president's official
  car or the president's official plane.

    Mr. Mujica was born into a poor family in Uruguay in 1935. His father died
when he was seven, and his mother supported the family. When he was a university
student, the (4.   ) of his country was in a bad condition and the difference of
quality of life between the rich and the poor was large. He decided to do something to
help his country. After he graduated from university, he (5.   ) against the
government. He was (6.   ) several times, but he never lost hope. He was finally
released in 1985 and became a politician ten years later. In 2009, he was (7.   )
president of Uruguay.

Part 2

Why did Jose Mujica come to be called "the poorest president in the world"? What does
he think about that?

1 Laundry hangs outside the house. Water comes from a well in a yard full of tall
grass. Only two police officers and a dog keep (1.   ) outside. This is the house of
a former president of Uruguay, Jose Mujica. It is on a farm outside the (2.   ),
Montevideo.

2 Mujica went to work from this residence even during his (3.   ) as president.
He didn't want to move to the official residence when he was elected in 2009. He
(4.   ) most of his salary to charities. His monthly (5.   ) was about 1,000
dollars. It was very low for a leader of a country, so he was seen as "the poorest
president in the world."

3 "I'm called the poorest president, but I don't feel poor," Mujica says. "A president is
a high-level official who is elected to carry out his or her (6.   ). A president is not
a king, not a god. A president is a civil servant. The ideal way of living is to live like
the (7.   ) of people."

Part 3

4 In April 2016, Mujica was invited to Japan for the first time because a Japanese (1.　　　) had just begun to sell the book, *The Poorest President in the World*. He gave a speech to young Japanese people at Tokyo University of Foreign Studies. In his (2.　　　) clothes, he didn't look like someone who had been a president of a country for five years.

5 Mujica delivered a message about happiness and poverty. In his address, he (3.　　　) the importance of love for our happiness. He said that it is the most important thing in the world for us people. "If people cannot share the feeling of (4.　　　) with their family, friends or neighbors, they are poor. The greatest poverty in this world is (5.　　　)."

6 According to Mujica, poverty is not about what we have or how much we have, not a matter of (6.　　　). "I'm not the poorest president. I can live well with what I have. The poorest person is the one who (7.　　　) a lot to live."

Part 4

7 Mujica thinks (1.　　　) of educating young people. As a politician, he believes that good education has the power to change the world in the future. Every time he visits a foreign country, he gives a speech to young people, especially (2.　　　) students.

8 In Tokyo, Mujica said that Japanese students should (3.　　　) themselves what happiness is and what poverty is. He told them that wealth is not what matters most, and that we should not spend all of our time worrying about (4.　　　) things. He stressed that life is not only about earning money. His words greatly impressed the young people of Japan.

9 Japan is a highly (5.　　　) country, and we are surrounded by various kinds of consumer goods and high-tech products. Japan has pursued economic (6.　　　) for decades, but many people say they are not satisfied. A survey shows that people's sense of happiness in Japan is not very high among the industrialized nations. Jose Mujica's message teaches us very important things about how we should think about (7.　　　).

Activity Plus

After a university student listened to Mujica's speech, he studied happiness in various countries. He made a report to present in class.

The United Nations has (1.　　　) the World Happiness Report every year since 2012. It is a survey of the state of global happiness, and it (2.　　　) more than 150 countries by their happiness levels.

The (3.　　　) of happiness in this report comes from several kinds of data: GDP per person, healthy life expectancy, and data from 1,000 people in each country about happiness. The questions ask people to rate several parts of their lives by using numbers from zero to ten. Zero is the worst possible life and ten is the best. The (4.　　　) are the results from some of the past few years.

Three or four of the top five each year are Northern (5.　　　) countries. They are thought to be the most highly developed welfare countries in the world. Most people in these countries feel that they are healthy, (6.　　　) and happy.

On the other hand, Japan ranks much lower (7.　　　) happiness. It is the lowest among the G7 nations. Japan is one of the (8.　　　) countries in some ways, for example, in economy and technology. However, Japanese people do not rank very high for feeling healthy, comfortable and happy. What is important for us to feel happy?

Part 1 　教科書 p.104〜p.105 　　/54

A Write the English words to match the Japanese. 【知識・技能（語彙）】（各2点）

1. .... 图 ブログ B1
2. .... 形 氷で冷やした
3. .... 图 ストロー B1
4. .... 图 少し A2
5. .... 图 スプーン A2
6. .... 形 環境に優しい

B Choose the word whose underlined part's sound is different from the other three.

【知識・技能（発音）】（各2点）

1. ア. b<u>l</u>og　　　イ. b<u>ou</u>ght　　　ウ. l<u>o</u>cal　　　エ. str<u>aw</u>
2. ア. <u>c</u>ompany　　イ. <u>c</u>ustomer　　ウ. pla<u>s</u>tic　　エ. <u>s</u>omething
3. ア. ic<u>ed</u>　　　イ. look<u>ed</u>　　　ウ. serv<u>ed</u>　　エ. stopp<u>ed</u>

C Complete the following English sentences to match the Japanese.

【知識・技能（表現・文法）】（完答・各3点）

1. その像はブロンズでできている。

   The statue (　　　　) (　　　　) (　　　　) bronze.
2. 市は全世帯に広報紙を提供している。

   The city (　　　　) public relations paper (　　　　) all households.
3. 彼女は今朝からまったく食べ物を口にしていない。

   She hasn't eaten food (　　　　) (　　　　) since this morning.

D Arrange the words in the proper order to match the Japanese.

【知識・技能（表現・文法）】（各4点）

1. その本は学校の図書室で借りられる。

   The book (can / borrowed / be / from) the school library.

   ----
2. 先生は生徒たちに英語で小論文を書かせた。

   The teacher (the students / the essay / write / made) in English.

   ----
3. 木のスプーンを使ってみたが，プラスチックのスプーンと違いを感じなかった。

   When I used a wooden spoon, (difference / felt / from / I / no / plastic one).

E Fill in each blank with a suitable word from the passage.

【思考力・判断力・表現力（内容）】（各5点）

1. The blogger thought that the paper straw would soon get wet and soft, but it was actually very (　　　　).
2. Seattle hopes to reduce plastic (　　　　).
3. Paper straws are (　　　　) and useful.

Part 2　教科書 p.106　　/54

A Write the English words to match the Japanese. 【知識・技能（語彙）】（各2点）

1. _____ 動 頼る，依存する A2　　2. _____ 動 …を見積もる,推定する B1

3. _____ 動 …を汚す，汚染する A2　4. _____ 動 とどまる A2

5. _____ 图 源，供給源 A2　　　　6. _____ 動 …を飲み込む A2

B Choose the word whose stressed syllable is different from the other three.

【知識・技能（発音）】（各2点）

1. ア．gar-bage　　　イ．land-fill　　　ウ．re-main　　　エ．sun-light

2. ア．pol-lute　　　イ．pro-duce　　　ウ．sup-ply　　　エ．swal-low

3. ア．dan-ger-ous　イ．dis-ap-pear　ウ．es-ti-mate　エ．pe-ri-od

C Complete the following English sentences to match the Japanese.

【知識・技能（表現・文法）】（完答・各3点）

1. 来年の冬，試験を受ける人の数は50万人以上と推定されている。

   It (　　　　) (　　　　) that more than 500,000 people will take the test next winter.

2. 昨日，熊谷市の温度は41度に達した。

   The temperature in Kumagaya City (　　　　) 41 degrees yesterday.

3. イタリアはたくさんの古い建物を見ることができる国だ。

   Italy is a country (　　　　) we can see many old buildings.

D Arrange the words in the proper order to match the Japanese.

【知識・技能（表現・文法）】（各4点）

1. 日本はエネルギー源を外国に依存している。

   Japan (depends / energy sources / for / foreign countries / on).

   _____

2. その実験で水は酸素と水素に分解された。

   In the experiment, (broken / down / into / the water / was) oxygen and hydrogen.

   _____

3. だれもタイムカプセルを埋めた場所を覚えていなかった。

   No one (buried / remembered / the place / the time capsule / we / where).

   _____

E Fill in each blank with a suitable word from the passage.

【思考力・判断力・表現力（内容）】（各5点）

1. Plastic waste can (　　　　) from the land into the ocean.

2. Plastics in the sea never (　　　　).

3. (　　　　) materials stick to the microplastics.

Part 3 教科書 p.107

/54

A Write the English words to match the Japanese. 【知識・技能（語彙）】（各2点）

1. _____ 名 生物学者
2. _____ 動 出血する B1
3. _____ 動 …を消化する
4. _____ 名 飢餓，餓死 B2
5. _____ 名 消化器官 B2
6. _____ 名 危険性，恐れ B1

B Choose the word whose underlined part's sound is different from the other three.

【知識・技能（発音）】（各2点）

1. ア．digest　　イ．influence　　ウ．instead　　エ．result
2. ア．customer　イ．full　　　　ウ．gut　　　　エ．stomach
3. ア．garbage　　イ．part　　　　ウ．starvation　エ．turtle

C Complete the following English sentences to match the Japanese.

【知識・技能（表現・文法）】（完答・各3点）

1. 5Gテクノロジーはビッグデータの高速輸送を可能にします。

   5G technologies make (　　　　) possible (　　　　) transfer big data quickly.
2. 彼は常にスマートフォンをチェックしている。

   He is checking his smartphone (　　　　) (　　　　) (　　　　).
3. 前大統領が心臓発作で死去しました。その結果，新しい大統領が選出されました。

   The former president (　　　　) (　　　　) a heart attack. (　　　　) a result, a new president was elected.

D Arrange the words in the proper order to match the Japanese.

【知識・技能（表現・文法）】（各4点）

1. 私は誤って重要なデータが入ったファイルを消去してしまった。

   I deleted a file that (by / contained / data / important / mistake).

   ----
2. 授業開始前に校庭から野球のベースを引き抜いておいてください。

   (before / from / pull out / the bases / the ground) the class begins.

   ----
3. 工事の騒音で学生は授業に集中するのが難しかった。

   Construction noise (difficult / focus / for / it / made / students / to) on their lessons.

E Fill in each blank with a suitable word from the passage.

【思考力・判断力・表現力（内容）】（各5点）

1. Sea animals cannot (　　　　) plastics in their stomachs.
2. We humans can also be (　　　　) by plastics in the sea.
3. The possible (　　　　) to food safety and our health are still not known.

Part 4 　教科書 p.110　／52

A　Write the English words to match the Japanese.　【知識・技能（語彙）】（各2点）

1. .... 图 炭素 B2
2. .... 動 溶け合う B1
3. .... 图 酸素 B1
4. .... 動 …を促進する B1
5. .... 图 払戻金 B1

B　Choose the word whose underlined part's sound is different from the other three.

【知識・技能（発音）】（各2点）

1. ア．b<u>u</u>siness　　イ．d<u>i</u>oxide　　ウ．enviro<u>n</u>ment　　エ．recy<u>c</u>le
2. ア．c<u>ar</u>bon　　イ．p<u>ar</u>t　　ウ．superm<u>ar</u>ket　　エ．w<u>or</u>k
3. ア．alth<u>ough</u>　　イ．contr<u>o</u>l　　ウ．c<u>ou</u>ntry　　エ．prom<u>o</u>te

C　Complete the following English sentences to match the Japanese.

【知識・技能（表現・文法）】（完答・各3点）

1. その建物は周りの雰囲気と溶け込んでいる。

   The building (　　　　) (　　　　) the surrounding atmosphere.
2. 私たちが先生から聞いたことは，来週試験があるということでした。

   (　　　　) we heard from the teacher was that we'll have an exam next week.
3. 学校にある公衆電話はもはや使われていません。

   Public phones at school are (　　　　) (　　　　) in use.

D　Arrange the words in the proper order to match the Japanese.

【知識・技能（表現・文法）】（各4点）

1. 試験の結果は完璧ではなかったが，合格ラインには達していた。

   The test result wasn't perfect, (although / had / it / reached / the passing line).

   ....

2. 彼女は運転免許証の取得に成功した。

   She (a driver's license / getting / in / successful / was).

   ....

3. あなたの評価はあなたがこれまで何をしたかによってだけではなく，何をしようとするかでも決まります。

   Your evaluation (depends / done / have / not / on / only / what / you) so far, but also on what you are going to do.

   ....

E　Fill in each blank with a suitable word from the passage.

【思考力・判断力・表現力（内容）】（各5点）

1. One solution to plastic pollution is to use "(　　　　)" plastics.
2. Another solution is (　　　　).
3. (　　　　) the amount of plastics we use seems to be important.

53

Activity Plus

教科書 p.114〜p.115　　／54

A　Write the English words to match the Japanese.　　【知識・技能（語彙）】（各2点）

1. ＿＿＿＿＿＿＿ 图 発見 B1　　2. ＿＿＿＿＿＿＿ 图 酵素

3. ＿＿＿＿＿＿＿ 图 過程, 処理, 作業 B1　4. ＿＿＿＿＿＿＿ 形 表面の

5. ＿＿＿＿＿＿＿ 图 組織, 構造 A2　　6. ＿＿＿＿＿＿＿ 形 実用的な, 効果的な B1

B　Choose the word whose underlined part's sound is different from the other three.

【知識・技能（発音）】（各2点）

1. ア. disc<u>o</u>very　　イ. h<u>u</u>ndred　　ウ. pr<u>o</u>cess　　エ. str<u>u</u>cture

2. ア. bac<u>t</u>eria　　イ. be<u>tt</u>er　　ウ. develo<u>p</u>　　エ. <u>t</u>est

3. ア. en<u>z</u>yme　　イ. <u>o</u>riginal　　ウ. re<u>c</u>ycle　　エ. var<u>i</u>ety

C　Complete the following English sentences to match the Japanese.

【知識・技能（表現・文法）】（完答・各3点）

1. 何百人もの新入生が毎年この学校に入学してくる。

(　　　　) (　　　　　　) new students enter this school every year.

2. この夏休みに, 弟はこの地域の昆虫の調査をした。

My brother (　　　　　) (　　　　　) insects in this area this summer vacation.

3. 多くの新薬はまずネズミで試験される。

Many new medicines are (　　　　　) (　　　　　) rats first.

D　Arrange the words in the proper order to match the Japanese.

【知識・技能（表現・文法）】（各4点）

1. 彼女は実験中に偶然新しい細菌を発見した。

She (by / the new bacteria / chance / discovered) during the experiment.

＿＿＿＿＿＿＿＿＿＿＿＿＿＿＿＿＿＿＿＿＿＿＿＿＿

2. その店に立ち寄るたびにポイントが加算されます。

Points are added (each / the store / time / visit / you).

＿＿＿＿＿＿＿＿＿＿＿＿＿＿＿＿＿＿＿＿＿＿＿＿＿

3. 外国から来たボランティアの人たちのおかげで, 大会をうまく終えることができた。

(countries / foreign / from / thanks / the volunteers / to), we were able to finish the event successfully.

＿＿＿＿＿＿＿＿＿＿＿＿＿＿＿＿＿＿＿＿＿＿＿＿＿

E　Fill in each blank with a suitable word from the passage.

【思考力・判断力・表現力（内容）】（各5点）

1. A group of scientists has developed a new (　　　　　) from "PET-eating" bacteria.

2. They hope that future (　　　　　) of PETase can work on other kinds of plastics.

3. PETase could be a (　　　　　) to the problem of recycling plastics.

総合問題

Read the following passage and answer the questions below.

What can we do to stop plastic pollution?　One solution is to use "biodegradable" plastics.　They can break down into water and carbon dioxide (CO_2) and finally blend with the environment.　However, they may not work in that way in dark, cool and low-oxygen places, such as in the sea.　For that reason, biodegradable plastics may not be the best solution, although they can be part of it.

(　1　) solution is recycling.　Some countries are successful in (A)promote it.　In Norway, for example, people can return plastic bottles to supermarkets and get a refund for them.　(B)This system has pushed the country's plastic bottle recycling rate to over 95 percent.　Across the world, however, only 9 percent of (C)use plastics are recycled.

(　2　) seems important, then, is (D)cut the amount of plastics we use.　To achieve (E)this, many businesses around the world are no (　3　) using single-use plastics.　Plastic waste control is not only about how we should make and recycle plastics.　(F)It is also about how we should use plastics.

1.　空所(1), (2), (3)に入る適切な語を選びなさい。　【知識・技能（語彙・表現）】（各4点）
　(1)　ア．Another　　イ．Any　　　　ウ．Some　　　エ．Special
　(2)　ア．It　　　　　イ．Something　ウ．That　　　エ．What
　(3)　ア．less　　　　イ．long　　　　ウ．longer　　エ．more

2.　下線部(A), (C), (D)の語を適切な形に変えなさい。　【知識・技能（文法）】（各4点）
　(A) (　　　　　　　　)　　(C) (　　　　　　　　)　　(D) (　　　　　　　　)

3.　下線部(B), (E), (F)が指す内容を日本語で説明しなさい。　【思考力・判断力・表現力（内容）】（各6点）
　(B)　--
　(E)　--
　(F)　--

4.　本文の内容に合っているものをすべて選びなさい。　【思考力・判断力・表現力（内容）】（完答・8点）
　ア．No country has succeeded in recycling plastics.
　イ．In Norway, if you take an empty plastic bottle to the store, you can get another one.
　ウ．In Norway, the recycling rate of PET bottles is over 95%.
　エ．Most companies should use single-use plastics.
　オ．Plastic waste control can be solved only by recycling plastics.

ディクテーション

Listen to the English and write down what you hear.

You want to learn something about Seattle. You have found the following blog post.

Hello from Seattle!

Oct 5, 2020

I stopped for coffee at a café. This was an iced coffee served there. Look at the straw. It was made of (1.   ), not plastic!

At first, I was a bit afraid that it would soon get wet and soft, but there was no problem at all. The paper straw was actually very (2.   ). I felt no difference from a plastic straw!

Why didn't the café use plastic straws? Seattle hopes to reduce plastic (3.   ). The city has now made local food service businesses stop using plastic straws, spoons, forks and knives. They can't provide them to customers anymore. Instead, they have to use something (4.   ). Paper straws are good for this purpose.

In addition, paper straws can have many different (5.   ). They can be printed with a variety of colors and letters. Companies can use them for their (6.   ). I don't think this is easy with plastic straws.

Paper straws are eco-friendly and really (7.   ). I hope more will be used in other places in the future.

Plastics have made our lives more convenient, but plastic waste is now a global problem and is getting more and more serious.

1 Our lives largely (1.   ) on plastics. They are used for many everyday goods: shopping bags, office supplies and even clothes. From 1950 to 2015, about 8.3 billion tons of plastics were (2.   ). About half of that amount was produced in the last 13 years of that period, and people are producing more and more plastics every year.

2 What happens after we throw plastics away? Some are burned as (3.   ), but most end up as waste in landfills or in the natural environment. In 2015, the amount of plastic garbage around the world reached about 6.3 billion tons. Such plastic waste can (4.   ) from the land into the ocean. The amount is estimated to be more than eight million tons each year.

3 However, that is not the end of the story. Plastics in the sea never (5.   ). They continue to pollute our water. Sunlight and waves break them down into smaller (6.   ). In addition, dangerous materials stick to these microplastics in the environment. These plastic bits remain in the places where many food sources are found. They can be eaten or (7.   ) by sea life.

Part 3

④ In Costa Rica, a biologist tries to pull out a plastic (1.   ) from a sea turtle's nose. The turtle is bleeding, and it appears to be in a lot of (2.   ). Perhaps it ate the straw by mistake and then tried to throw it up. Instead of getting out of its mouth, the straw went into its nose.

⑤ Sea animals, including fish and shellfish, can mistake plastics for food and swallow them. The chances are higher for microplastic pieces. The animals cannot (3.   ) plastics in their stomachs, and they feel full all the time. This makes it difficult for them to eat actual food. As a result, many animals in the sea are dying of (4.   ).

⑥ We humans can also be (5.   ) by plastics in the sea. Scientists believe that microplastics are present in seafood. Most of them seem to (6.   ) in the guts of fish and shellfish. It appears that they do not move into the parts we eat. However, the possible (7.   ) to food safety and our health are still not known.

Part 4

⑦ What can we do to stop plastic (1.   )? One solution is to use "biodegradable" plastics. They can break down into water and carbon dioxide (CO_2) and finally (2.   ) with the environment. However, they may not work in that way in dark, cool and low-oxygen places, such as in the (3.   ). For that reason, biodegradable plastics may not be the best solution, although they can be part of it.

⑧ Another solution is (4.   ). Some countries are successful in promoting it. In Norway, for example, people can return plastic bottles to supermarkets and get a refund for them. This system has (5.   ) the country's plastic bottle recycling rate to over 95 percent. Across the world, however, only 9 percent of used plastics are recycled.

⑨ What seems important, then, is (6.   ) the amount of plastics we use. To achieve this, many businesses around the world are no longer using single-use plastics. Plastic waste (7.   ) is not only about how we should make and recycle plastics. It is also about how we should use plastics.

Activity Plus

You are doing some research on the plastic-waste problem. On the Internet, you have found an article about a discovery made by a group of scientists.

Can Plastic-Eating Bacteria Save the Earth?

Back in 2016, "PET-eating" (1.   ) were found. PET is a plastic widely used in drink bottles. Now a group of scientists has developed a new enzyme from the bacteria. It can break PET down more quickly. While PET takes hundreds of years to (2.   ) down in nature, the enzyme, called PETase, can start the process in just a few days.

The (3.   ) came by chance when the scientists were looking into the enzyme. They found that the performance of PETase could be improved by changing its surface structure. The improved enzyme was also (4.   ) on another plastic, PEF. This plastic is also slow to break down in nature. The result was surprising. The enzyme worked better on PEF than on PET. The scientists are now trying to make the enzyme work even better. They hope that future (5.   ) can work on other kinds of plastics.

PETase could be a solution to the problem of recycling plastics. Plastic materials lose some (6.   ) each time they are recycled. Bottles become clothes, then carpets, and finally, waste. The recycling circle is not closed. However, PETase may be able to close the circle. It can turn plastics back into their (7.   ) materials. Thanks to this, plastics may be used again and again without losing quality. Although this technology hasn't reached practical use yet, it may give us a (8.   ) about how to solve the plastic waste problem.

Part 1

教科書 p.120〜p.121

/54

A　Write the English words to match the Japanese.　【知識・技能（語彙）】（各2点）

1. _____ 图 語り部, 物語を話す人 B1　2. _____ 图 支持者, 支援者, 主張者

3. _____ 图 入場, 入場料 B1　4. _____ 動 …を破壊する, 滅ぼす A2

5. _____ 图 副操縦士　6. _____ 图 後悔, 遺憾, 悲しみ A2

B　Choose the word whose stressed syllable is different from the other three.

【知識・技能（発音）】（各2点）

1. ア．de-stroy　　イ．pi-lot　　ウ．post-er　　エ．sto-ry

2. ア．e-vent　　イ．per-son　　ウ．re-ceive　　エ．re-gret

3. ア．a-chieve-ment　イ．ad-mis-sion　ウ．ad-vo-cate　エ．a-tom-ic

C　Complete the following English sentences to match the Japanese.

【知識・技能（表現・文法）】（完答・各3点）

1. お母さんはいつもぼくに怒っているんだ。

   My mother is always (　　　　) (　　　　) me.

2. 私たちは今の状況をよく考えるべきだ。

   We should (　　　　) (　　　　) our present situation.

3. 彼女はフランス語ではなくてイタリア語を勉強しています。

   She studies (　　　　) French (　　　　) Italian.

D　Arrange the words in the proper order to match the Japanese.

【知識・技能（表現・文法）】（各4点）

1. 一生懸命勉強する人は成功するだろう。

   (hard / study / succeed / those / who / will).

   _____

2. 校則についてのきみたちの考えを聞かせてくれますか。

   (can / me / share / with / you / your thoughts) on school rules?

   _____

3. 私は，彼が本当は何を言いたかったのかがわかった。

   I realized (he / really / say / to / wanted / what).

   _____

E　Fill in each blank with a suitable word from the passage.

【思考力・判断力・表現力（内容）】（各5点）

1. Koko Kondo will talk about her (　　　　) at the International Center in Tokyo.

2. She has received many prizes for her excellent work as a peace (　　　　).

3. A chance to see the co-pilot of the plane that dropped the atomic bomb (　　　　) her life.

Part 2 　教科書 p.122

/54

A　Write the English words to match the Japanese.　【知識・技能（語彙）】（各2点）

1. _____ 形 核の，原子力の B1　2. _____ 動 言及する，口に出す A2

3. _____ 動 …を許す B1　4. _____ 動 …を生き残る A2

5. _____ 名 犠牲者 B1　6. _____ 形 医療の，内科の A2

B　Choose the word whose stressed syllable is different from the other three.

【知識・技能（発音）】（各2点）

1. ア．pas-tor　　　イ．re-fer　　　ウ．vic-tim　　　エ．weap-on

2. ア．a-live　　　イ．for-give　　　ウ．in-jure　　　エ．sur-vive

3. ア．char-ac-ter　イ．im-por-tance　ウ．med-i-cal　　エ．nu-cle-ar

C　Complete the following English sentences to match the Japanese.

【知識・技能（表現・文法）】（完答・各3点）

1. そのテレビ番組は子供たちに悪い影響を及ぼすかもしれない。

   That TV program may (　　　) a bad (　　　) on children.

2. プレゼンテーションで，私はSDGs に言及するつもりです。

   In my presentation, I will (　　　) (　　　) SDGs.

3. 晴れていたら，テニスができるのになあ。

   If it (　　　) fine, we (　　　) play tennis.

D　Arrange the words in the proper order to match the Japanese.

【知識・技能（表現・文法）】（各4点）

1. 彼のEメールアドレスを知っていれば，連絡を取ることができるのに。

   If I (contact / could / his email address, / I / knew) him.

2. 先生は私たちに自分の経験を伝えた。

   Our teacher (on / passed / his experience / to / us).

3. 先日，私の友達は部屋の掃除を手伝ってくれた。

   (clean / helped / me / my friends / my room) the other day.

E　Fill in each blank with a suitable word from the passage.

【思考力・判断力・表現力（内容）】（各5点）

1. In May 2016, Barack Obama visited Hiroshima and (　　　) a speech there.

2. He (　　　) to a woman who had forgiven a pilot who dropped the atomic bomb.

3. Koko's father was a famous pastor who (　　　) the bombing.

Part 3 教科書 p.124

/54

A Write the English words to match the Japanese. 【知識・技能 (語彙)】(各2点)

1. _____ 副 幸運にも, 幸いなことに A2   2. _____ 名 後遺症

3. _____ 動 …のかたきを討つ   4. _____ 副 密かに, 内緒で B1

5. _____ 動 …を噛む, …に噛みつく B1   6. _____ 副 激しく, 痛烈に B2

B Choose the word whose underlined part's sound is different from the other three.

【知識・技能 (発音)】(各2点)

1. ア. b<u>i</u>te   イ. b<u>i</u>tterly   ウ. v<u>i</u>ctim   エ. v<u>i</u>sit

2. ア. aftereff<u>e</u>ct   イ. regr<u>e</u>t   ウ. s<u>e</u>cretly   エ. t<u>e</u>rrible

3. ア. act<u>u</u>ally   イ. feat<u>u</u>re   ウ. fort<u>u</u>nately   エ. terr<u>i</u>bly

C Complete the following English sentences to match the Japanese.

【知識・技能 (表現・文法)】(完答・各3点)

1. もっと勉強しておけば, 試験に合格できたのに。

   If I had studied harder, I could (   ) (   ) the exam.

2. 彼の変な服装を見て笑わずにはいられなかった。

   I couldn't (   ) (   ) at his strange clothes.

3. 多くの人々が飢餓に苦しんでいる。

   Many people are (   ) (   ) starvation.

D Arrange the words in the proper order to match the Japanese.

【知識・技能 (表現・文法)】(各4点)

1. 私たちはたくさんの人々が病院に入るのを見ました。

   We (enter / many / people / saw / the hospital).

   _____

2. 彼はそのパーティーに行ったことを後悔している。

   (going / he / regrets / the party / to).

   _____

3. もし私が彼の電話番号を知らなかったら, だれも彼に連絡できていなかっただろう。

   If I hadn't known his telephone number, (contacted / could / have / him / nobody).

   _____

E Fill in each blank with a suitable word from the passage.

【思考力・判断力・表現力 (内容)】(各5点)

1. Koko's family survived the (   ) although they had to face the terrible realities.

2. She appeared on a TV show (   ) her father in America.

3. After she saw the pilot's eyes filled with tears, she (   ) he was also a victim.

Part 4 　教科書 p.125

/52

A Write the English words to match the Japanese. 【知識・技能（語彙）】（各2点）

1. .... 图 必要性 B2
2. .... 图 一生の仕事，ライフワーク
3. .... 图 恐怖 A2
4. .... 動 消えていく，薄れる B1
5. .... 图 責任 B1

B Choose the word whose stressed syllable is different from the other three.

【知識・技能（発音）】（各2点）

1. ア．hor-ror　　イ．e-vent　　ウ．fu-ture　　エ．lat-er
2. ア．be-gin-ning　イ．med-i-cal　ウ．mem-o-ry　エ．re-al-ize
3. ア．ac-tiv-i-ty　イ．ex-pe-ri-ence　ウ．gen-er-a-tion　エ．ne-ces-si-ty

C Complete the following English sentences to match the Japanese.

【知識・技能（表現・文法）】（完答・各3点）

1. その計画に賛成の人もいれば，反対の人もいます。

   (　　　　) of them are for the plan and (　　　　) are against it.
2. その時計はおじいさんが私に残してくれたものです。

   That clock was (　　　　) (　　　　) to me from my grandfather.
3. 私たちの記憶はやがて消えていきます。

   Our memories will (　　　　) (　　　　) gradually.

D Arrange the words in the proper order to match the Japanese.

【知識・技能（表現・文法）】（各4点）

1. これは私が今までに唯一登った山です。

   This is the only mountain (climbed / ever / have / I / that).

   ----

2. この城にはこれまでに多くの人が訪れました。

   This castle (a lot of / been / by / has / people / visited).

   ----

3. そのとき地図を持っていたら，迷わなかったかもしれないのに。

   If we had had a map at that time, (have / lost / might / not / our way / we).

E Fill in each blank with a suitable word from the passage.

【思考力・判断力・表現力（内容）】（各5点）

1. Koko's lifework as a storyteller had started because she realized it is necessary to (　　　　) the memory of the war.
2. The experiences of the *hibakusha* need to be (　　　　) with future generations.
3. We will no longer be able to hear the living (　　　　) of the *hibakusha*.

Activity Plus 　教科書 p.128〜p.129

/54

A　Write the English words to match the Japanese.　【知識・技能（語彙）】（各2点）

1. ＿＿＿＿＿＿＿＿　图 討論，討議 A2
2. ＿＿＿＿＿＿＿＿　图 定義，定義づけ B1
3. ＿＿＿＿＿＿＿＿　動 異なる，違う B1
4. ＿＿＿＿＿＿＿＿　動 …を定義する B1
5. ＿＿＿＿＿＿＿＿　形 逆の，正反対の A2
6. ＿＿＿＿＿＿＿＿　形 平和な，穏やかな A2

B　Choose the word whose stressed syllable is different from the other three.

【知識・技能（発音）】（各2点）

1. ア．a-gree　　　イ．de-fine　　　ウ．dif-fer　　　エ．re-fer
2. ア．ac-ci-dent　　イ．dif-fi-cult　　ウ．dis-cus-sion　　エ．op-po-site
3. ア．def-i-ni-tion　イ．dic-tio-nar-y　ウ．per-son-al-ly　エ．for-tu-nate-ly

C　Complete the following English sentences to match the Japanese.

【知識・技能（表現・文法）】（完答・各3点）

1. もし私たちに十分な時間があれば，あなたに会いに行くのですが。

If we (　　　　) enough time, we would go to see you.

2. 動物の好みは人によってちがう。

Personal preferences of animals can (　　　　) from person to person.

3. クラスのほとんどはあなたの意見に反対しているけれど，私はあなたの意見に賛成です。

Although most of our classmates disagree, I (　　　　) with your idea.

D　Arrange the words in the proper order to match the Japanese.

【知識・技能（表現・文法）】（各4点）

1. その学生は宿題をすることは勉強の一部だと定義しています。

That student (as / defines / doing / homework / part of / study).

＿＿＿＿＿＿＿＿＿＿＿＿＿＿＿＿＿＿＿＿＿＿＿＿＿＿

2. 私たちみんなが彼の意見に賛成しているわけではありません。

(agree / all / his opinion / not / of / us / with).

＿＿＿＿＿＿＿＿＿＿＿＿＿＿＿＿＿＿＿＿＿＿＿＿＿＿

3. 私は彼の言ったことがまったく理解できなかった。

I (at / could / he / not / said / understand / what) all.

＿＿＿＿＿＿＿＿＿＿＿＿＿＿＿＿＿＿＿＿＿＿＿＿＿＿

E　Fill in each blank with a suitable word from the passage.

【思考力・判断力・表現力（内容）】（各5点）

1. The (　　　　) of peace can differ among people.
2. Mika defines peace as a state of having the (　　　　) for life.
3. Emily feels that peace is not something (　　　　) at all.

総合問題

/50

Read the following passage and answer the questions below.

Two atomic bombs were dropped on Japan in August 1945. About 140,000 people in Hiroshima and about 70,000 people in Nagasaki had died by the end of the year. Seventy-one years later, in May 2016, Barack Obama became the first sitting president to visit Hiroshima. He made a speech there and told the world the importance of (1) up nuclear weapons.

In his speech, President Obama referred to a woman (A)(a pilot / dropped / had forgiven / the atomic bomb / who / who) on Hiroshima. The woman's name is Koko Kondo. She has shared her story as a *hibakusha*, a surviving victim of the atomic bombings. Obama's speech (B)(gain / helped / her activities / worldwide recognition).

Koko's father, Kiyoshi Tanimoto, was a famous pastor who also survived the bombing. He is one of the main characters in *Hiroshima*, a book (C)write by John Hersey. The war left many young women (D)injure by the atomic bomb. Kiyoshi helped them receive medical care in the United States. He had a great influence (2) Koko. If he (3) alive now, what would he say to his daughter?

1. 空所(1), (2), (3)に入る適切な語を選びなさい。　　　　【知識・技能（語彙・表現）】（各4点）

   (1)　ア．gave　　　　イ．give　　　　ウ．given　　　　エ．giving

   (2)　ア．at　　　　イ．of　　　　ウ．on　　　　エ．with

   (3)　ア．had　　　　イ．is　　　　ウ．were　　　　エ．will be

2. 下線部(A), (B)の（　　　）内の語句を適切に並べかえなさい。　　【知識・技能（文法）】（各4点）

   (A)　..

   (B)　..

3. 下線部(C), (D)の語を適切な形に変えなさい。　　　　　　　　【知識・技能（文法）】（各3点）

   (C)（　　　　　　　）　(D)（　　　　　　　）

4. 本文の内容に合っているものをすべて選びなさい。　　【思考力・判断力・表現力（内容）】（完答・8点）

   ア．Barack Obama was the first American sitting president to visit Hiroshima.

   イ．President Obama referred to a woman who had forgiven the pilot who flew the plane that dropped the atomic bomb.

   ウ．Koko Kondo has never forgiven what the Americans did to Hiroshima.

   エ．Kiyoshi Tanimoto died in August 1945.

   オ．Kiyoshi wrote a book named *Hiroshima*.

5. 次の問いの答えになるよう，空所に適切な語を補いなさい。

   【思考力・判断力・表現力（内容）】（完答・各8点）

   (1)　What happened in May 2016?

   ―― Barack Obama visited Hiroshima and (　　　　　)(　　　　　)(　　　　　).

   (2)　How long did it take for American president to visit Hiroshima for the first time after World War II?

   ―― It took (　　　　　) years.

ディクテーション

Listen to the English and write down what you hear.

Part 1

You are walking on a street. You find a poster of an interesting event.
The International Center in Tokyo will host a special talk.
Living with Hiroshima: My Memories

　　　Koko Kondo was born in Hiroshima in 1944. She (1.　　　) the atomic bombing when she was just eight months old. After she grew up, Koko became a (2.　　　). She has shared her own experiences with a lot of people, from small children to older people. She gives her talks both in Japanese and in English. She has received many prizes for her excellent work as a peace (3.　　　).

1:30 p.m. on Saturday, July 2, 2022　　　　Building K, Room 303
Admission Free　　　　　　　　　　　　Information: 0123-45-xxxx
https://www.ictokyo.ac.jp/peace
About the Talk

　　　After World War II, Koko remained (4.　　　) with those who destroyed Hiroshima. However, a chance to see an American man changed her life. He was the co-pilot of the plane that dropped the atomic bomb on Hiroshima. When she saw his deep (5.　　　), Koko realized what she really hated was not the person in front of her but war itself. Her story gives us a chance to (6.　　　) on our thoughts about war.

Part 2

Why do the *hibakusha* talk about the war? What can we learn from them? What stories need to be passed on to the next generations?

1　(1.　　　) atomic bombs were dropped on Japan in August 1945. About 140,000 people in Hiroshima and about 70,000 people in Nagasaki had died by the end of the year. Seventy-one years later, in May 2016, Barack Obama became the first (2.　　　) president to visit Hiroshima. He made a speech there and told the world the importance of giving up nuclear weapons.

2　In his speech, President Obama referred to a woman who had (3.　　　) a pilot who dropped the atomic bomb on Hiroshima. The woman's name is Koko Kondo. She has shared her story as a *hibakusha*, a surviving (4.　　　) of the atomic bombings. Obama's speech helped her activities gain worldwide (5.　　　).

3　Koko's father, Kiyoshi Tanimoto, was a famous pastor who also survived the bombing. He is one of the main (6.　　　) in *Hiroshima*, a book written by John Hersey. The war left many young women injured by the atomic bomb. Kiyoshi helped them receive (7.　　　) care in the United States. He had a great influence on Koko. If he were (8.　　　) now, what would he say to his daughter?

Part 3

4　Fortunately, Koko's family survived the bombing, although they had to face the terrible (1.　　　) of the war. They saw many people come to their church: women with terrible burns on their faces, children who had lost their families, and people suffering from the (2.　　　) of the bomb. At that time, Koko couldn't help thinking, "If the Americans had not dropped the atomic bomb, we wouldn't have gone through this terribly (3.   ) experience."

⑤ Koko had long wanted to avenge the victims, and a chance actually came when she was ten years old. She got the chance to visit America and appear on a TV show (4.   ) her father. The program secretly planned a (5.   ) between her family and Captain Robert Lewis, the co-pilot of the Enola Gay.

⑥ At first, Koko thought she would kick and bite Lewis, but the next moment, she was surprised to see the pilot's eyes filled with (6.   ). He remembered the bombing and said, "My God, what have we done?" He bitterly regretted (7.   ) out the bombing order. In that moment, Koko realized the pilot was also a victim of war.

Part 4

⑦ That important (1.   ) changed Koko's way of thinking. She wrote in her book later, "If I had not met Captain Robert Lewis, I might have become a person who never forgives others." She then began to realize the necessity of spreading the memory of the war from person to person. This was the (2.   ) of her lifework as a storyteller and peace advocate.

⑧ The stories told by the *hibakusha*, including Koko's, have been received in many ways by younger people. Some of them have also become new storytellers who hand down the stories of the *hibakusha*. Others try to express the (3.   ) of war by painting, acting or giving music performances. They all believe that the experiences of the *hibakusha* need to be shared with future (4.   ).

⑨ Someday, we will no longer be able to hear the living (5.   ) of the *hibakusha*. However, the memories of August 6 and 9, 1945, must never fade away. As Japan is the only (6.   ) that has ever suffered atomic bomb attacks, each of us has a responsibility to hand down the memories of the war to future generations. In the future, how will you (7.   ) what you know about war?

Activity Plus

You are listening to a discussion about the definition of peace.

Teacher: The definition of peace can (1.   ) among us. A dictionary may define it as a state or period without war. If so, the opposite word of peace will be war. However, not all of us agree with this (2.   ) as we may not feel peaceful even when we are not fighting each other. How would you define peace? Discuss it in your group.

Mika: I define peace as a state of having the (3.   ) for life. If we didn't have enough food, clothing and housing, it would be difficult to live. Having the necessities for life is the basis of peace, I believe.

Satoshi: I agree with Mika, but I also think of peace as a state of being safe. Nobody wants to have car (4.   ). Nobody wants to be attacked when they are walking at night. Safety must be part of peace. What do you think, Emily?

Emily: Um, personally, I feel peaceful when I'm having a meal with my family or talking with my friends. That is not something (5.   ) at all. Just being able to spend a normal life means peace to me.

Satoshi: I like your idea, Emily. Although we don't usually (6.   ) that, we may have peace already in our life.

Part 1 教科書 p.134〜p.135

/46

A Write the English words to match the Japanese. 【知識・技能（語彙）】（各2点）

1. _____ 動 …をインストールする B1　2. _____ 图 領収書 A2

B Choose the word whose underlined part's sound is different from the other three.

【知識・技能（発音）】（各2点）

1. ア．autom<u>a</u>tically　イ．inst<u>a</u>ll　ウ．smartph<u>o</u>ne　エ．th<u>ou</u>ght
2. ア．conv<u>e</u>nience　イ．inst<u>ea</u>d　ウ．r<u>ea</u>der　エ．rec<u>ei</u>pt
3. ア．appli<u>c</u>ation　イ．<u>c</u>ouple　ウ．lun<u>ch</u>　エ．mon<u>ey</u>

C Complete the following English sentences to match the Japanese.

【知識・技能（表現・文法）】（完答・各3点）

1. 新発売のスマートフォンを買うためにたくさんの人が並んだ。

   Many people stood (　　　　) (　　　　) to buy the newly released smartphone.
2. 夕食代は私が支払います。

   I will (　　　　) (　　　　) dinner.
3. 数か月の訓練の後，彼は運転免許を取得した。

   He got his driver's license after a (　　　　) (　　　　) months of training.

D Arrange the words in the proper order to match the Japanese.

【知識・技能（表現・文法）】（各4点）

1. あなたがどのようにしてここに来たのか，教えてください。

   (came / here / how / me / tell / you).

   ----

2. 私は買い物をするコンビニエンスストアで，いつもはデジタルマネーを使う。

   I usually use digital money (at / convenience / I / shop / store / the / where).

   ----

3. 領収書が届いたことを確認してください。

   Please (arrived / has / make / your receipt / sure / that).

E Fill in each blank with a suitable word from the passage.

【思考力・判断力・表現力（内容）】（各5点）

1. At *Amazing Supermarket*, you don't have to (　　　　) in line to pay for your shopping.
2. You can bring your smartphone with you instead of (　　　　).
3. You can (　　　　) the items you want into your shopping bag and just walk out with them.

Part 2

教科書 p.136〜p.137

/54

A Write the English words to match the Japanese. 　　　　【知識・技能（語彙）】（各2点）

1. _____ 形 人工の，人工的な A2
2. _____ 名 知能, 理解力, 思考力 A2
3. _____ 動 …を認める，許す A2
4. _____ 名 感知装置，センサー
5. _____ 副 一方では B1
6. _____ 動 …を取り除く, 除外する B1

B Choose the word whose stressed syllable is different from the other three.

【知識・技能（発音）】（各2点）

1. ア．ac-count　　　イ．ma-chine　　　ウ．re-move　　　エ．sen-sor
2. ア．cash-less　　　イ．col-lect　　　ウ．i-tem　　　エ．no-tice
3. ア．es-ca-la-tor　　イ．in-ter-est-ed　ウ．su-per-mar-ket　エ．tech-nol-o-gy

C Complete the following English sentences to match the Japanese.

【知識・技能（表現・文法）】（完答・各3点）

1. AI 技術に興味を持ったので，彼はそれを学べる大学に進学した。

   (　　　) (　　　) in AI technology, he went to a university where he could study it.

2. 会議の前にこのデータに目を通しておいていただけますか。

   Could you (　　　) (　　　) this data before the meeting?

3. 明日オーストラリアに出発する準備はできていますか。

   (　　　) you (　　　) (　　　) leave for Australia tomorrow?

D Arrange the words in the proper order to match the Japanese.

【知識・技能（表現・文法）】（各4点）

1. 子供たちが眠っている間に，彼は木の下にプレゼントを置いた。

   (his children / sleeping / were / while), he put some presents under the tree.

   _____

2. スマートフォンが落ちていたので，拾って交番に届けた。

   I found a smartphone on the ground, so I (and / it / it / picked / to / took / up) the police box.

   _____

3. 部屋でラジオを聞いていたとき，外で奇妙な音が聞こえた。

   (in / listening / my room / the radio / to), I heard a strange noise outside.

   _____

E Fill in each blank with a suitable word from the passage.

【思考力・判断力・表現力（内容）】（各5点）

1. You see a colorful (　　　) in your morning newspaper.
2. At *Amazing Supermarket*, you need to touch your (　　　) on the phone reader at the entrance.
3. The devices tracking you all over the store (　　　) the items you pick up.

A Write the English words to match the Japanese.　【知識・技能（語彙）】（各2点）

1. ＿＿＿＿＿＿ 形 進歩した,先進の,高度の A2　2. ＿＿＿＿＿＿ 名 観点 B1

3. ＿＿＿＿＿＿ 動 …を見分ける,識別する B1　4. ＿＿＿＿＿＿ 形 かすかな,とらえにくい B2

5. ＿＿＿＿＿＿ 名 教育,指図,命令 B1　6. ＿＿＿＿＿＿ 名 自動操作,オートメーション

B Choose the word whose underlined part's sound is different from the other three.

【知識・技能（発音）】（各2点）

1. ア. based　　イ. basic　　ウ. number　　エ. subtle

2. ア. human　　イ. incoming　　ウ. jump　　エ. sudden

3. ア. automation　　イ. graph　　ウ. patient　　エ. shape

C Complete the following English sentences to match the Japanese.

【知識・技能（表現・文法）】（完答・各3点）

1. 兄は大学を卒業し，一人で暮らしている。

   My brother has graduated from college and is living (　　　) (　　　).

2. 彼の成功は経験に基づいている。

   His success (　　　) (　　　) (　　　) his experience.

3. AI は自動車や翻訳機，掃除機のような，私たちの周りのいろいろな物に使われている。

   AI has been used in a variety of things around us, (　　　) (　　　) automobiles, translators and cleaners.

D Arrange the words in the proper order to match the Japanese.

【知識・技能（表現・文法）】（各4点）

1. 毎年多数の生徒がこのプログラムに参加します。

   (a / in / number / of / part / students / take / this program) every year.

   ----

2. 私は彼を彼の双子の兄と区別することができなかった。

   I wasn't (able / distinguish / from / him / his / to / twin brother).

   ----

3. フランス語を話せるようになるのに2年かかりました。

   It took (French / learn / me / speak / to / to / two years).

E Fill in each blank with a suitable word from the passage.

【思考力・判断力・表現力（内容）】（各5点）

1. Some fields AI has been introduced into are basic, while others are more (　　　).

2. At the machine learning stage, AI is given a (　　　) to tell the apples from the oranges.

3. Deep learning has made AI different from a simple (　　　) tool.

Part 4 教科書 p.140

/54

A Write the English words to match the Japanese. 【知識・技能（語彙）】（各2点）

1. .... 名 発明家 B2
2. .... 形 想像力に富んだ, 創造的な A2
3. .... 動 …に取って代わる A2
4. .... 動 交流する, 触れ合う B1
5. .... 動 …を欠いている, 持っていない B2
6. .... 名 可能性, 潜在能力 B1

B Choose the word whose stressed syllable is different from the other three.

【知識・技能（発音）】（各2点）

1. ア. ex-change   イ. ex-cuse   ウ. in-vent   エ. is-land
2. ア. com-put-er   イ. fa-vor-ite   ウ. in-com-ing   エ. in-ter-est
3. ア. col-or-ful   イ. de-ci-sion   ウ. i-de-a   エ. po-ten-tial

C Complete the following English sentences to match the Japanese.

【知識・技能（表現・文法）】（完答・各3点）

1. テニスのこととなると, だれも彼に勝つことはできない。

   (   ) (   ) (   ) to playing tennis, no one can beat him.

2. 子供たちは有名な選手と交流してうれしそうだった。

   The children seemed happy to (   ) (   ) the famous players.

3. トムは, 旅行会社に勤めているのですが, 私の娘の留学の旅行手配を手伝ってくれました。

   Tom, (   ) (   ) for a travel agency, helped my daughter set up travel arrangements for her studying abroad.

D Arrange the words in the proper order to match the Japanese.

【知識・技能（表現・文法）】（各4点）

1. ゴッホの作品は, 昔に描かれたものだが, 今でも人気がある。

   Van Gogh's works, (ago / long / painted / were / which), are still very popular.

   ----

2. ぜひ春に日本に来てください。（春には）美しい桜の花が見られますよ。

   Please come to Japan in spring, (beautiful / can / cherry blossoms / see / when / you).

   ----

3. 彼は人間と動物が共存できる社会を作ろうとしています。

   He is trying to create a society (and animals / can / go / hand / hand / in / human beings / where).

E Fill in each blank with a suitable word from the passage.

【思考力・判断力・表現力（内容）】（各5点）

1. In the future, AI may (   ) (   ) jobs from human beings.
2. AI can never (   ) artists and inventors because AI is not creative.
3. AI has huge (   ) to make our future brighter.

Activity Plus 教科書 p.144～p.145 　　/54

A　Write the English words to match the Japanese.　【知識・技能（語彙）】（各2点）

1. .... 形 音声の A2　　2. .... 图 翻訳, 解釈 B2

3. .... 副 特に B1　　4. .... 图 農業 B1

5. .... 图 産業, 工業 B1　6. .... 動 …を収穫する, 取り入れる A2

B　Choose the word whose stressed syllable is different from the other three.

【知識・技能（発音）】（各2点）

1. ア．com-plete-ly　　イ．con-di-tion　　ウ．de-part-ment　　エ．hap-pen-ing

2. ア．en-vi-ron-ment　　　　　イ．in-tel-li-gence
   ウ．tech-nol-o-gy　　　　　　エ．trans-por-ta-tion

3. ア．au-to-mat-ic　　イ．Ca-na-di-an　　ウ．mys-ter-i-ous　　エ．suc-cess-ful-ly

C　Complete the following English sentences to match the Japanese.

【知識・技能（表現・文法）】（完答・各3点）

1. 母は毎朝父を駅まで車で送っています。

   My mother (　　　　) my father (　　　　) the station every morning.

2. AI は輸送や農業といったような分野で導入されています。

   AI has been introduced into (　　　　) fields (　　　　) transportation and agriculture.

3. 仕事を楽しみと結びつけるのは難しい。

   It is difficult to (　　　　) business (　　　　) pleasure.

D　Arrange the words in the proper order to match the Japanese.　【知識・技能（表現・文法）】（各4点）

1. 明日何が起こるかはだれもわからない。

   (happen / knows / no / one / tomorrow / what / will).

   ----

2. タブレットを持っていれば，学生は重い教科書を持ち運ぶことも不要になります。

   Students (anymore / carry / don't / have / heavy / textbooks / to) if they have tablets.

   ----

3. ここはスマートフォンを使って買い物ができるスーパーマーケットです。

   This is (a supermarket / can / shop / where / you) with your smartphone.

E　Fill in each blank with a suitable word from the passage.

【思考力・判断力・表現力（内容）】（完答・各5点）

1. Words such as "(　　　　) recognition" and "machine (　　　　)" are known in the field of communication technology.

2. AI makes medical tools and medical care much smarter and more patient-(　　　　).

3. AI decides on the best moment for planting seeds and (　　　　) crops.

総合問題

／50

Read the following passage and answer the questions below.

You see a colorful advertisement in your morning newspaper. While you are looking it over, your eyes stop on this sentence: "No waiting in line to pay (1) your shopping." (A)(getting / in / interested / new / store / this), you decide to buy some things there.

Before you go to *Amazing Supermarket*, you need to download an application onto your smartphone. This is necessary in order to create your account and allow cashless shopping in the store. When you arrive at the supermarket, you need to touch your smartphone on the phone reader at the entrance. Then your shopping record becomes active and you are ready to do your shopping.

Although you may not notice, while you are shopping, many small cameras and sensors which have different purposes are tracking you all over the store. These devices sense the items you pick up and automatically add (B)them to your smartphone shopping list. (2), any item you return to its shelf is removed from the list. You think, "I understand! This is AI!" You (C)(have / heard / just / remembered / the news / you) a few days ago. "AI is operating this store," the news (3).

1. 空所(1), (2), (3)に入る適切な語を選びなさい。 【知識・技能（語彙・表現）】（各4点）

   (1) ア. at　　　　　イ. for　　　　　ウ. in　　　　　エ. to

   (2) ア. During　　　イ. Meanwhile　　ウ. Sometimes　　エ. While

   (3) ア. read　　　　イ. said　　　　　ウ. told　　　　　エ. wrote

2. 下線部(A), (C)の (　　) 内の語句を適切に並べかえなさい。 【知識・技能（文法）】（各4点）

   (A) --

   (C) --

3. 下線部(B)が指す具体的な内容を本文中から抜き出しなさい。 【思考力・判断力・表現力（内容）】（6点）

   (B) --

4. 本文の内容に合っているものをすべて選びなさい。 【思考力・判断力・表現力（内容）】（完答・8点）

   ア. You decide to go to *Amazing Supermarket* because you don't want to wait in line.

   イ. Arriving at the supermarket, you have to download an application onto your smartphone at the entrance.

   ウ. If you have an account created with the application, you can enjoy shopping without bringing money.

   エ. You can't do your shopping if you don't touch your smartphone on the reader.

   オ. To return the items you put into your shopping bag, you should remove them from the list by yourself.

5. 次の問いの答えになるよう，空所に適切な語を補いなさい。【思考力・判断力・表現力（内容）】（完答・各8点）

   (1) Why is it necessary to download an application onto your smartphone before you go to *Amazing Supermarket*?

   　　—— To (　　　　　) your account and (　　　　　) cashless shopping in the store.

   (2) What is operating *Amazing Supermarket*?

   　　—— (　　　　　) is.

ディクテーション

Listen to the English and write down what you hear.

Part 1

One morning, you read an advertisement about a new supermarket. You go there and then listen to an announcement at the supermarket.

Welcome to *Amazing Supermarket*! Now Open in Your Town!

A (1.   ) new supermarket opens in your town today!

No need to bring (2.   ). No waiting in line to pay for your shopping.

Come and enjoy shopping at our first store in your town!

Here is how you shop at our supermarket:

1) Install the *Amazing Supermarket* application in your smartphone before you come.
2) Bring your (3.   ) with you instead of money.
3) Enter *Amazing Supermarket*. Touch your smartphone on the reader at the entrance.
4) Start your shopping. Put the items you want into your shopping bag. You can return them to their (4.   ) places if you change your mind.
5) Go back to the entrance where you came in, and just walk out with the items.
6) Check your smartphone after shopping. Your receipt will arrive soon after you leave *Amazing Supermarket*.

For more information, please contact us: https://www.amazingsupermarket.com

Tel.: (888)-550-xxxx Visit our first shop at 8th Street, Washington St. 22885.

Good morning, customers. Thank you very much for visiting *Amazing Supermarket* on opening day. Before you start shopping, just a couple of things to (5.   ).

When you (6.   ) your smartphone on the phone reader, please make sure that your *Amazing Supermarket* application has been started successfully. After you choose an item, if you decide to return it, please put it back in its original place.

We're having an opening sale for one week. All items are 20% off from our usual price, so don't (7.   ) this chance! Enjoy your shopping!

Part 2

AI, or artificial intelligence, is one of the hottest topics in our society today. Have you ever used AI technology? Have you ever been to places where AI technology is used?

1 You see a colorful (1.   ) in your morning newspaper. While you are looking it over, your eyes stop on this sentence: "No waiting in line to pay for your shopping." Getting interested in this new store, you (2.   ) to buy some things there.

2 Before you go to *Amazing Supermarket*, you need to download an (3.   ) onto your smartphone. This is necessary in order to create your account and allow cashless shopping in the store. When you arrive at the supermarket, you need to touch your smartphone on the phone reader at the entrance. Then your shopping (4.   ) becomes active and you are ready to do your shopping.

3 Although you may not notice, while you are shopping, many small cameras and (5.   ) which have different purposes are tracking you all over the store. These devices sense the items you pick up and automatically add them to your smartphone shopping (6.   ). Meanwhile, any item you return to its shelf is removed from the list. You think, "I understand! This is AI!" You have just remembered the news you heard a few days ago. "AI is (7.   ) this store," the news said.

Part 3

4 AI was created after World War II by a number of scientists, and it has been introduced into a variety of fields today. Some fields are (1.   ), while others are more advanced.

⑤ Image (2.⎽⎽⎽⎽⎽⎽), such as telling apples from oranges, is one example. First, the AI needs to learn just as we humans do. A number of apple and orange images are delivered to the AI. When the AI is given a "viewpoint," such as "color," to (3.⎽⎽⎽⎽⎽⎽) the apples from the oranges, then it learns to do so even with new incoming apple and orange images. This stage of learning is called "machine learning." At the more advanced stage called "deep (4.⎽⎽⎽⎽⎽⎽)," the AI learns to find viewpoints by itself. This is based on a large amount of information from outside. The AI then learns how to search for (5.⎽⎽⎽⎽) information about apples, such as their size, shape or quality, to separate them without any (6.⎽⎽⎽⎽) from human beings.

⑥ Deep learning is an essential part of AI because it has made AI different from a simple automation tool. With deep learning, AI can usually make the best decision, just as we humans do in our everyday (7.⎽⎽⎽⎽).

Part 4

⑦ After your new experience at *Amazing Supermarket*, a (1.⎽⎽⎽⎽) spreads in your mind: "In the future, will AI take over jobs from human beings?" To answer this question, you need to think about what AI is (2.⎽⎽⎽⎽) at doing than human beings and what you can do better than AI.

⑧ It is true that AI is better than you when it comes to (3.⎽⎽⎽⎽) for information from a huge amount of data and making the best decision. However, you have abilities which are unique to human beings. You can (4.⎽⎽⎽⎽) new ideas, and you can love things and people.

⑨ Artists and inventors are (5.⎽⎽⎽⎽). On this point, AI can never replace them. Doctors, childcare workers and teachers need to feel love toward the people they interact with in their jobs. AI, which (6.⎽⎽⎽⎽) this feeling, cannot do these types of jobs.

⑩ AI has huge potential to make our future brighter. It is our (7.⎽⎽⎽⎽) to create a good society where human beings and AI can go hand in hand together.

Activity Plus

You are at a special exhibition about AI. In front of you there are four exhibition sections for different fields. You are learning about the latest AI applications in each field.

Transportation: Can you imagine all the members of your family playing (1.⎽⎽⎽⎽), eating lunch, or watching videos while your family car drives you to your travel goal? No one is driving the car, but AI is! This is no longer a dream. Some companies are expecting (2.⎽⎽⎽⎽) self-driving AI cars in the near future.

Communication: Perhaps you have heard such words as "audio recognition" and "machine translation." These technologies became possible through deep-learning AI. Your foreign language (3.⎽⎽⎽⎽) can be supported by these technologies when you need to communicate with people in different countries, particularly for such (4.⎽⎽⎽⎽) as business meetings or traveling abroad.

Healthcare: AI makes medical tools and medical care much smarter and more patient-specific. AI (5.⎽⎽⎽⎽) data from many sources and combines it with big data. Doctors can use the data to give faster and better care. Elderly patients at many (6.⎽⎽⎽⎽) homes don't have to go to the hospital anymore.

Agriculture: Agriculture is an industry where AI is used widely. AI plays three main important roles; (7.⎽⎽⎽⎽) small flying machines to take care of farming products, monitoring soil conditions, and (8.⎽⎽⎽⎽) farming environments to decide on the best moment for planting and harvesting.

Part 1 　教科書 p.150〜p.151 　　/52

A Write the English words to match the Japanese. 　【知識・技能（語彙）】（各2点）

1. .... 图 刑務所，監獄 B1　2. .... 動 …を盗む A2

3. .... 图 刑事，探偵 B1　4. .... 形 筋骨たくましい，運動競技の B1

5. .... 動 …を下げる，低くする B2

B Choose the word whose underlined part's sound is different from the other three.

【知識・技能（発音）】（各2点）

1. ア. l<u>ow</u>er　　　イ. <u>o</u>nly　　　ウ. st<u>o</u>len　　　エ. th<u>ou</u>ght

2. ア. <u>a</u>nother　　イ. b<u>a</u>nk　　　ウ. m<u>o</u>ney　　　エ. y<u>ou</u>ng

3. ア. aftern<u>oo</u>n　イ. f<u>u</u>ll　　　ウ. s<u>ui</u>tcase　　エ. thr<u>ou</u>gh

C Complete the following English sentences to match the Japanese.

【知識・技能（表現・文法）】（完答・各3点）

1. 彼はテレビ番組でよい意見を言うことで有名です。

   He is (　　　　) (　　　　) giving good opinions on TV shows.

2. 彼女はその国で初の女性首相になる政治家のように見えます。

   She (　　　　) (　　　　) a politician who will be the first female prime minister of the country.

3. その医者はまず診察のため彼女の口の中をのぞき込んだ。

   The doctor first (　　　　) (　　　　) her mouth for an examination.

D Arrange the words in the proper order to match the Japanese.

【知識・技能（表現・文法）】（各4点）

1. ホセ・ムヒカは刑務所から解放され，ついには大統領になった。

   (and / finally became / from / Jose Mujica / prison / released / was) the president.

   ----

2. 窓はとても重く，壊して開けなければならなかった。

   The window was (break / had / heavy / it / open / so / that / to / we).

   ----

3. 彼は仕事中なので私の電話に気付かないかもしれない。

   He (and / at / is / may / not / notice / work) my phone call.

E Fill in each blank with a suitable word from the passage.

【思考力・判断力・表現力（内容）】（各5点）

1. After he was (　　　　) from prison, Jimmy Valentine stole much money.

2. Ben Price was a detective who was trying to (　　　　) Jimmy.

3. Jimmy and a young lady first met in a small (　　　　) named Elmore.

Part 2   教科書 p.152〜p.153   /52

A   Write the English words to match the Japanese.   【知識・技能（語彙）】（各2点）

1. _____ 動 …のふりをする, …を装う A2   2. _____ 名 態度, 物腰 A2

3. _____ 形 心地よい, 感じのよい A2   4. _____ 名 身元, 正体 B1

5. _____ 名 結婚式 A2

B   Choose the word whose stressed syllable is different from the other three.

【知識・技能（発音）】（各2点）

1. ア. no-tice   イ. pleas-ant   ウ. pre-tend   エ. suit-case

2. ア. at-tack   イ. im-press   ウ. man-ner   エ. re-main

3. ア. com-mu-ni-ty イ. i-den-ti-ty   ウ. im-por-tant-ly エ. in-for-ma-tion

C   Complete the following English sentences to match the Japanese.

【知識・技能（表現・文法）】（完答・各3点）

1. 大学卒業後，その兄弟は出版社を設立しました。

   After graduating from university, the brothers (   ) (   ) a publishing company.

2. 明日の便の窓側の席を予約したいのですが。

   I (   ) (   ) to reserve a window seat for tomorrow's flight.

3. この夏にできるだけ多くの本を読みなさい。

   In this summer, read as (   ) (   ) (   ) you can.

D   Arrange the words in the proper order to match the Japanese.

【知識・技能（表現・文法）】（各4点）

1. 私は昨日，ジャックが池の周りを走っているのを見ました。

   I (around / Jack / running / saw / the pond) yesterday.

   _____

2. 英語の先生は私たちに日本語で話さないようにと言った。

   The English teacher (in / Japanese / not / speak / to / told / us).

   _____

3. 何度も意見交換をしているうちに，私たちはお互いの考えを理解するようになった。

   After exchanging opinions many times, we (to / thoughts / understand / got / each other's).

   _____

E   Fill in each blank with a suitable word from the passage.

【思考力・判断力・表現力（内容）】（各5点）

1. The hotel clerk gave Jimmy much information because Jimmy's clothes and (   ) are impressive.

2. People in Elmore wanted a good (   ) shop.

3. Jimmy and Annabel Adams fell in (   ) and started to plan their wedding.

Part 3 　教科書 p.154〜p.155 　/44

A Write the English words to match the Japanese. 【知識・技能（語彙）】（各2点）

1. .... 名 銀行家，銀行業者 B2

B Choose the word whose underlined part's sound is different from the other three.
【知識・技能（発音）】（各2点）

1. ア．shoe　　イ．suit　　ウ．tool　　エ．touch
2. ア．breakfast　イ．member　ウ．secretly　エ．wedding
3. ア．another　イ．family　ウ．money　エ．something

C Complete the following English sentences to match the Japanese.
【知識・技能（表現・文法）】（完答・各3点）

1. 彼女はコンピュータの不調の原因がわかった。

She (　　　　) (　　　　) the cause of the trouble with her computer.

2. 宿題を提出することを忘れましたよね？

You forgot to submit your assignment, (　　　　) (　　　　)?

3. 彼女は使い終わった参考書を友人に譲り渡した。

She (　　　　) her used reference book (　　　　) to her friend.

D Arrange the words in the proper order to match the Japanese.
【知識・技能（表現・文法）】（各4点）

1. ジミーは釈放された後でさえ，お金を盗むのをやめなかった。

Jimmy (didn't / even after / finish / he / money / stealing / with) was released.

2. 彼は駅へ行く途中で図書館に寄った。

He stopped (at / on / the library / the station / the way / to).

3. 新企画が成功すると確信していますか。

(about / are / of / sure / the success / you) the new project?

E Fill in each blank with a suitable word from the passage.
【思考力・判断力・表現力（内容）】（各5点）

1. Jimmy wrote a letter in order to give his (　　　　) away to his friend.
2. A few days after the letter was sent, Ben Price (　　　　) in Elmore.
3. Jimmy left for the bank along with several members of the Adams (　　　　).

Part 4 教科書 p.156〜p.157 /54

A Write the English words to match the Japanese. 【知識・技能（語彙）】（各2点）

1. _____ 图 (銀行窓口の)現金出納係 B1　　2. _____ 图 金切り声，悲鳴 A2

3. _____ 圖 しっかりと，堅く B1　　4. _____ 图 暗闇，闇 B1

5. _____ 图 恐怖，恐れ，不安 A2　　6. _____ 形 必死の，絶望的な B1

B Choose the word whose underlined part's sound is different from the other three.

【知識・技能（発音）】（各2点）

1. ア. d<u>ar</u>kness　　イ. f<u>ir</u>mly　　ウ. h<u>ar</u>d　　エ. st<u>ar</u>t

2. ア. br<u>ea</u>kfast　　イ. d<u>e</u>sperate　　ウ. scr<u>ea</u>m　　エ. t<u>e</u>ller

3. ア. m<u>o</u>ther　　イ. <u>o</u>pen　　ウ. s<u>o</u>n　　エ. t<u>o</u>uch

C Complete the following English sentences to match the Japanese.

【知識・技能（表現・文法）】（完答・各3点）

1. 私の母は弁護士の兄を誇りに思っています。

   My mother (　　　　) (　　　　) (　　　　) her brother, who is a lawyer.

2. 私は誤って知らない人に電話をかけてしまった。

   I called a stranger (　　　　) (　　　　).

3. 少しの間待っていただければ，スミス氏に会うことができます。

   If you wait (　　　　) (　　　　) (　　　　), you can meet Mr. Smith.

D Arrange the words in the proper order to match the Japanese.

【知識・技能（表現・文法）】（各4点）

1. あなたは私たちがテニスの大会で優勝した日のことを覚えていますか。

   (do / remember / the day / we / when / won / you) the tennis tournament?

   _____

2. カーテンが引いて開けられ，私は目が覚めた。

   (and / I / open / pulled / the curtains / were) woke up.

   _____

3. その女優はそのときすてきなドレスを着ていたのですが，私の部屋の前に現れました。

   The actress, then (a / appeared / dress, / wearing / wonderful) in front of my room.

   _____

E Fill in each blank with a suitable word from the passage.

【思考力・判断力・表現力（内容）】（各5点）

1. The new safe in the Elmore Bank was as large as a small (　　　　).

2. The woman screamed because Agatha was (　　　　) the safe and the door couldn't
   be opened.

3. Mr. Adams told everyone in the room to be (　　　　) because he heard the sound
   of the child's voice.

Part 5　教科書 p.158〜p.159　　/54

A　Write the English words to match the Japanese.　【知識・技能（語彙）】（各2点）

1. ＿＿＿＿＿＿＿ 形 絶望的な　　2. ＿＿＿＿＿＿＿ 名 ベスト，チョッキ

3. ＿＿＿＿＿＿＿ 名 鋼鉄（製の）B1　4. ＿＿＿＿＿＿＿ 形 疲れ切った，へとへとの B1

5. ＿＿＿＿＿＿＿ 動 ためらう，躊躇する B1　6. ＿＿＿＿＿＿＿ 動 …に見覚えがある，…を認める B1

B　Choose the word whose stressed syllable is different from the other three.

【知識・技能（発音）】（各2点）

1. ア．de-spair　　イ．min-ute（名詞）　ウ．smooth-ly　　エ．some-thing

2. ア．dis-ap-pear　イ．hes-i-tate　　ウ．rec-og-nize　　エ．si-lent-ly

3. ア．at-ten-tion　イ．com-plete-ly　ウ．mis-tak-en　　エ．un-der-stand

C　Complete the following English sentences to match the Japanese.

【知識・技能（表現・文法）】（完答・各3点）

1. 少し暑いです。窓を開けてくれませんか。

It's a little hot. Open the window, (　　　　) (　　　　)?

2. 山道を運転していたとき，大きな石が行く手に立ちはだかっていた。

When I was driving down a mountain, a big stone stood (　　　) (　　　) (　　　).

3. その医者は80歳で引退した。そのときから，島に医者はいない。

The doctor retired at the age of 80. (　　　) that time (　　　), there has been no doctor on the island.

D　Arrange the words in the proper order to match the Japanese.　【知識・技能（表現・文法）】（各4点）

1. 議長が欠席したときは，副議長が議長の代わりをします。

When the chairperson is absent, (his or her / place / take / the vice-chairperson / will).

----

2. テスト期間中，私たちは職員室から離れているように言われた。

During the exam period, (away / from / stay / the teachers' room / to / told / we / were).

----

3. 私の書いたことがだれかの感情を害してしまうかもしれないと心配した。

I (afraid / hurt / I / was / what / would / wrote) someone's feelings.

E　Fill in each blank with a suitable word from the passage.

【思考力・判断力・表現力（内容）】（完答・各5点）

1. Annabel believed that Jimmy could open the (　　　　) of the safe and save Agatha.

2. There were (　　　　) for opening safes in Jimmy's suitcase.

3. Ben (　　　　) away and walked down the street instead of arresting Jimmy.

総合問題

/50

Read the following passage and answer the questions below.

　Annabel turned to Jimmy.　Her large eyes were full of pain, but not yet despairing. A woman believes that the man she loves can find a way to do anything.　"Can't you do something, Ralph?　Try, won't you?"　He looked at her with a strange, soft smile on his lips and in his eyes.

　"Annabel," he said, "give me that rose you are wearing, will you?"

　She couldn't understand what he meant, but she put the rose in his hand.　Jimmy took it and placed it in the pocket of his vest.　Then he threw off his coat.　With that act, Ralph D. Spencer disappeared, and (A)Jimmy Valentine took his place.　"Stay away from the door, all of you," he ordered.

　He placed his suitcase on the table and opened it.　From that time on, he didn't (B)(any / anyone / attention / pay / to) else there.　Quickly he (C)lay the strange shining tools on the table.　Nobody moved as they watched him work.　Soon Jimmy's drill was biting smoothly into the steel door.　In ten minutes ── faster than he had ever done it before ── he opened the door.

　Agatha, completely exhausted but unharmed, ran into her mother's arms.　Jimmy Valentine silently put his coat back on and walked toward the front door of the bank. As he went, he thought he heard a voice call, "Ralph!"　But he never hesitated.　At the door, a big man was standing in his way.　"Hello, Ben!" said Jimmy.　"You're here at last, (1) you?　Well, let's go.　I don't care now."

　"I'm afraid (D)you're mistaken, Mr. Spencer," said Ben Price.　"I don't believe I recognize you."　Then the big detective turned away and walked slowly down the street.

1.　空所(1)に入る適切な語を選びなさい。　　　　　　　　【知識・技能（語彙・表現）】（6点）

　　ア．are　　　　　　　　イ．aren't　　　　　ウ．do　　　　　　エ．don't

2.　下線部(A)の具体的な内容を選びなさい。　　　　　　　【思考力・判断力・表現力（内容）】（10点）

　　ア．金庫破りになる　　　イ．銀行家になる　　　ウ．刑事になる　　　エ．新郎になる

3.　下線部(B)の（　　　）内の語句を適切に並べかえなさい。　　　【知識・技能（文法）】（8点）

　　- -

4.　下線部(C)の語を適切な形に変えなさい。　　　　　　　　【知識・技能（文法）】（6点）

　　（　　　　　　　）

5.　下線部(D)に関して，何が間違いなのか，適切なものを選びなさい。

　　　　　　　　　　　　　　　　　　　　　　　　　　　　【思考力・判断力・表現力（内容）】（10点）

　　ア．ジミーがアナベルと結婚すること　　　　イ．ジミーが銀行家になること

　　ウ．ジミーが逮捕されると思っていること　　エ．ジミーが見逃してもらえると思っていること

6.　本文の内容に合っているものをすべて選びなさい。　【思考力・判断力・表現力（内容）】（完答・10点）

　　ア．Annabel believed that Jimmy could save Agatha.

　　イ．When Jimmy threw off his coat, Ralph D. Spencer took his place.

　　ウ．Inside the suitcase were the strange shining tools.

　　エ．When the door was finally opened, Agatha, completely exhausted, was sleeping.

　　オ．Ben Price succeeded in arresting Jimmy at last.